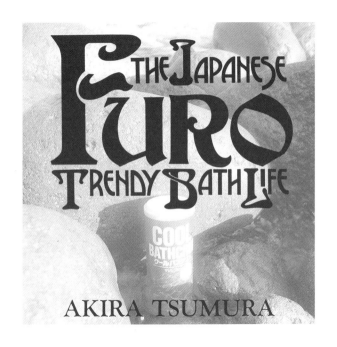

THE JAPANESE
FURO
TRENDY BATH LIFE

AKIRA TSUMURA

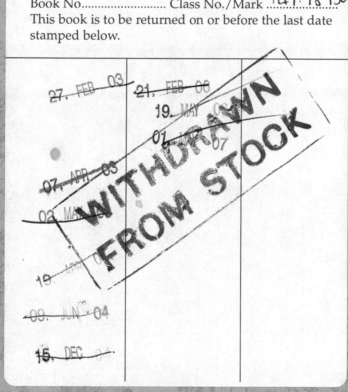

FURO

THE JAPANESE TRENDY BATH LIFE

AKIRA TSUMURA

Japan Publications, Inc.

Editorial Direction: Tetsuo Yoshioka (Random, Inc.)
Editors: Hajime Shirai, Lei Ujika
Photographer: Masayuki Hayashi
Designers: Kazuo Ikegami, Hiromi Terasawa

747.78TSU

Published by Japan Publications, Inc., Tokyo and New York

Distributors:
UNITED STATES: Kodansha America, Inc. through Farrar,
Straus & Giroux, 19 Union Square West, New York 10003.
CANADA: Fitzhenry & Whiteside Ltd., 195 Allstate Parkway,
Markham, Ontario, L3R 4T8. BRITISH ISLES & EUROPEAN
CONTINENT: Premier Book Marketing Ltd., 1 Gower Street,
London WC1E 6HA. AUSTRALIA & NEW ZEALAND:
Bookwise International, 54 Crittenden Road, Findon, South Australia
5023. THE FAR EAST & JAPAN: Japan Publications Trading
Co., Ltd., 1–2–1, Sarugaku-cho, Chiyoda-ku, Tokyo 101.

First Edition: April 1992
ISBN: 0–87040–875–5
LCCC: No. 91-076148

Printed in Japan

TABLE OF CONTENTS

PREFACE 6

CHAPTER I
THE TRENDY BATH LIFE 9

Contemporary Bathrom Design 10
The Bathroom as Living Room:
   The Nunoi Residence 11
A Bath Life of Amenity:
   The Shimono Residence 14
Traditional Beauty:
   The Yano Residence 18
An Aquatic Life:
   The Suzuki Residence 21
After Gaudi: Echo Timber 24
On the Seaside of Mediterranean Sea:
   The Ukita Residence 28
What's Going on the Bathrooms of These
   Major People? 31
   Ms Manami Fuji (actress) 32
   Yukiko Hanai (fashion designer) 35
The Author's Bath
   Art Deco Drama: Akira Tsumura 38
How do Foreigners Enjoy Japanesque Bath
   Life? 46
   An Old-Fashioned Japanese Bath:
      Mr. Wilk and Dr. Precker 48
   A Bathroom Like a Movie Set:
      Agnes Guibout 52
Communication in the Whirlpool 56
   Whirlpool Party:
      The Kanazawa Residence 57
   The Relaxing Life Style of a Home
      Worker: Naozo Sugimoto 60
   Bath Time for Ecologists:
      Pension Alm 63

Bath Resorts 66
The New Wave Country Club:
   Southern Cross Resort 67
Kurhaus: Mer Club 69
A Trendy Sports Club: Spatz 71
Andree Putman's Hotel: Le Lac 73
Japan's Finest Hot Spring Inn:
   Yagyu No Sho 78
A Renowned Spa in a Natural Setting:
   Taiseikan 84

Body Care and Bath Fashion 86
Futuristic Beauty:
   Shu Uemura Esthetic Salon 89
For a Beautiful Bath:
   The Body & Bath Shop 90
Lovely Bath Accessories 93
Designer's Bath Fashions 96
Bath Powders 98
The Herbal Bath 99
Potpurri 100

CHAPTER II
A HISTORY OF THE JAPANESE
   BATH 101

Born Bathers 102
The Steam Bath Tradition 104
Buddhism and Bathing 108
The History of Sento 112
The Pleasure of Bathing 116
Houseguests and the Bath 118
Home Baths 120

CHAPTER III
THE EFFICACY OF
   BATHING 125

Bath life for a Comfortable Life 126
The Science of Bathing and Health 127
Physical Characteristics and
   Effects of Bathing 128
Bathing for Fresh-Looking Skin 130
Bathing to Recover a Healthy Rhythm
   of Life 132
Bathing Additives to Make a Home Bath
   Like a Spa 133
"Medicated Baths" with Extracts of
   Unrefined Medicines 134

CHAPTER IV
PAINTINGS 135

CHAPTER V
UKIYOE 155

APPENDICES 177

PREFACE

Today the Japanese people are faced with the necessity of re-establishing a more easy-going lifestyle. To succeed, a physically comfortable and balanced environment must be created. Certainly, a restful bathing routine is a meaningful step toward such a more relaxed way of life.

In truth the bath has been an integral part of life in Japan for hundreds of years. The Japanese have long been adept at incorporating bathing within their daily schedules and, so doing, easing the vicissitudes of the day. The spa industry, established to provide resorts and medical treatment facilities, is another forte. Traditionally, baths have served as social centers which fostered communication among the populace, and even a cursory examination of artworks which depict scenes from ordinary life in days gone by makes this quite apparent. However, cultural aspects of the bath are undergoing massive change today.

Generally speaking, these changes are shifting bathing practices in the direction of increasing amenity and elegance. Bathroom design is becoming more sophisticated, more bath products are being used, people are increasingly concerned with body care, and, consequently, bathing is now exciting the attentions of growing numbers of Japanese. Moreover growing concerns regarding health in general are inciting greater involvement in bathing as part of a healthy lifestyle.

"The Japanese Trendy Bath Life" introduces these new aspects of the Japanese bath, and also explores the Japanese love of bathing throughout history. Employing the bath as a method of promoting good health is also discussed. Discover the world of the Japanese bath, and you will derive greater pleasure from your own bathing experience.

Chapter I
THE TRENDY BATH LIFE

Contemporary Bathroom Design

These days many Japanese magazines feature comfortable new bathroom designs as cover stories. Since a trendy bathroom can enrich one's everyday life, today's Japanese, whose basic interests are shifting from fashion to living, have chosen the bath as a new object of concern in their quest for a more satisfying life. What's more, now many seek the services of professional architects to design their residences, which results in more unique and sophisticated bathroom designs being produced.

The bathroom is today taking on additional characteristics which enable it to function as a living room. If it is to be a place for people to gather and enjoy their time together, the bathroom needs new concepts not limited to design but including other factors as well: private thermal spring water service, a high-tech AV system, artworks, and so on. All these are efforts to make the bath more inviting and comfortable. Creating bathrooms which are unrivaled in amenities is the object of contemporary bathroom design in Japan.

The Bathroom as Living Room: The Nunoi Residence

The first homeowner we introduce here is an internationally renowned management consultant who currently owns three residences: one in Tokyo, another at the highland spa resort of Hakone, and a third at Atami, a seaside hot spring resort on the Izu Penninsula southwest of Tokyo. Each is a "main" residence and as such he makes use of all three homes.

The house at Hakone was designed by *Shuji Miura*[1] shortly after he left Arata Isozaki Atelier to set up shop on his own. Miura designed it as an "intelligent house" so that the owner could easily access information in spite of its remove from Tokyo. Its facsimile machine, computer and parabolic antenna make it possible for simple office work to be accomplished at home. All rooms, including the bathroom and the lavatory, are provided with TV monitors so that the owner can obtain the latest information from anywhere in the house.

Futurologist *Alvin Toffler,*[2] in his book *"The Third Wave"*, predicted that "home workers" would multiply as a result of advances in information and communication technologies. The Nunoi residence is, in this light, an example of the housing of the near future. The number of home workers is mushrooming, especially in the United States, and Toffler's prediction seems to be coming to pass as the Third Millenium approaches.

The Nunoi home is completely equipped with an audio-visual system which can be controlled from any room. Even in the bathroom, television and audio can be manipulated by remote control. The main bathroom is supplied with hot water drawn from a natural hot spring. The bathtub is big enough for three people who, while relaxing in the bath, can conduct a business meeting either over the phone or in person.

This bathroom can provide the same functions as a living room. The trend toward such designs has appeared due to the increasing desire for multi-functional and amenity-filled bathrooms.

The Japanese have also become aware of the advantages of being a home worker. Today many executives understand that it is often more productive to work in a comfortable private space than at an office. Viewed from this perspective, the bathroom of the Nunoi residence offers a superb working environment. Contemplation while relaxing in the bath and enjoying the natural scenery outside the windows should facilitate more creative thinking. The Nunoi home is a demonstration of the style which bathrooms will assume in the near future.

(Kanagawa Prefecture)

The Nunoi residence has a postmodern look. On the left, an elevator tower, and on the right, the first floor bathroom with its slanting window. Above it on the second floor is a Japanese-style room. A living room is on the third floor and a bedroom on the fourth.

opposite: The bathroom which features a bathtub big enough for three. It is private hot spring and boasts body shower high tech equipment such as TV and sound system.

left: The living room which faces a wonderful view of grand Mt. Fuji. This is a futuristic room equipped with a thirty-seven inch video set, a concert-quality audio system, a computer and a facsimile machine.

right: A skylight which incorporates an automatic sun-shutter.

A Bath Life of Amenity: The Shimono Residence

"Wow! Life would be great if I could live in a house like this!" We anticipate that such an enthusiastic response would burst from any young woman upon being shown our second offering. This home may be the ideal dream house of Tokyo's young upper class. It has contemporary appeal.

The owner, Mr. Shimono, operates his own company and has two young children. He also has a sizable contemporary art collection, which supplies the finishing touch to the air of affluence which permeates this home. This house indeed expresses a trendy lifestyle in contemporary Japan.

Mr. Shimono inherited from his father an estate in a quiet residential area of central Tokyo. Subsequently, he solicited an architect to design an up-to-the moment residence and thus this home with its pleasant bathroom came into existance. It certainly is trendy and incorporates many fun ideas. The bath space is the amenity center here, and is the source of all entertainment elements. Beyond that, it also generates the feeling of comfort which this home exudes.

The most attractive aspect of this fascinating residence is the art collection. Some background: it is impossible to construct a traditional Japanese garden for an open-air bath in central Tokyo. The necessary space is prohibitively expensive, and even if it were possible many homeowners such as the Shimonos may simply lack interest in such traditional gardens. Rather, art collections are considered desirable today. The resulting explosion of art collecting in Japan is well-known abroad, and corporate collectors are paying enormous sums for the works of revered artists. However there are many private collectors as well, and almost every Japanese home has its art collection of some kind, large or small. Boasting a magnificent bathroom and an impressive art collection, the Shimono residence therefore is clearly representa-

tive of the trends in contemporary Japan.

The house has, in addition to its bathroom, a small garden done in white pebbles where works of art may be displayed. While admiring them, the Shimonos can soak in a soothing whirlpool bath. The bath is completely automatically controlled, and can even be operated from the kitchen by his wife. This high-tech convenience is yet another symbol of the Japan of today. Naturally television can be viewed from the bath, and even children, who ordinarily are less than fond of baths, love this one. They love the whirlpool, and they have TV as well. Adults can do light exercise in the attached training room, and a sauna bath awaits in yet another room. All of these amenities support improved health.

The bath facilities actually occupy most of the first floor—quite a unique use of space. In this regard, it is safe to say that the bathroom of the Shimono residence performs better as a living room than a conventional living room does. Thus, this home is quite a study in today's trends and in enjoyable bath life. *Pittori Piccoli*[3] did the design.

(Setagaya, Tokyo)

previous page, left: Training room in the Shimono residence.

previous page, right: A shower with a sauna beyond.

right: A bath area. Outside is a small garden in which art work is displayed. Watching TV in the bathtub is a pleasant way to spend one's bath time.

upper left: A dining room with a Japanese room beyond. The house features a floor heating system which extends to all rooms.

upper right: The living room.

lower: An exterior view.

Traditional Beauty: The Yano Residence

The third home we will look into has thirteen impressive Japanese- and Western-style rooms. Though the house is almost a year old, some of its rooms have never been used. There is certainly more than enough space for the Yanos with their two children. To have a residence like this is quite exceptional in Japan, where people often cannot afford enough space in which to live comfortably. Incidently, the lady of our third residence, Mrs. Yano, employs three maids, which is again a considerable rarity in this country. This sort of home is indeed gorgeous.

Architecturally, the home integrates traditional Japanese and Western influences. On the ground floor is a traditional Japanese-style room and a new Japanese-style garden. Most of the rooms are done in the Western-style, and the owners use chairs and beds in everyday life, but since the Japanese cannot abandon completely the aesthetic of their roots the Yano home has this Japanese-style room. Yet this gorgeous room has never been used, suggesting that traditional beauty is becoming merely one kind of decoration.

Of all the bathrooms in this house, the one constructed of black granite is the most striking. The mysterious brilliancy of this stone epitomizes the traditional Japanese concept of beauty. The blending of modern high-tech ideas with this ancient sensibility is unique. The bathroom has a "body shower," which is popular here due to its ability to knead and loosen the muscles. There is also a sauna bath meant to address deep health concerns. The design, which harmonizes traditional beauty and up-to-the-moment facilities, creates an unusually pleasant setting for the bath.

A bathroom in the Yano residence glimmers with the mysterious beauty of black granite.

upper left: A body shower for muscle massage.

upper right: A sauna.

left: A "citron bath"—Fresh herb baths are popular in Japan today. However, baths infused with citron and iris have long been enjoyed by the Japanese.

The Japanese wash themselves outside of the bathtub, and, while Western-style bath tools are now in common use, it is unthinkable that this custom could change. One first pours warm water over oneself, dipping it from the tub, and then eases into the bath. After resting in the tub and becoming warm, one gets out and washes thoroughly. In most cases this is followed by using the shower attachment hooked to the wall nearby the tub. Then, after rinsing off the soap, one again enters the bath to warm the body once more. This style of bathing is effective for health care and produces beneficial effects combating fatigue, rheumatism and other complaints.

Marble, an emblem of sumptuousness in the West, is not used for floors but for walls only in Japanese bathrooms. For this reason, and because of its superior performance and traditional beauty, black granite rather than marble is in Japan synonymous with the luxurious bath. *Junji Kawada*[4] did the design.

(Katsushika, Tokyo)

upper: The three-storied Yano residence. A Japanese garden lies between the entrance gate and the house.

lower: The Western style entrance hall.

An Aquatic Life: The Suzuki Residence

A synchronized swimming enthusiast occupies our fourth residence, which appears to have been designed for her private use. It boasts an eighteen meter swimming pool, rather large for a home pool. In this pool Mrs. Suzuki and her friends practice their synchronized swimming, complete with music, every day.

Mrs. Suzuki really is a lover of water. When a bit tired by swimming, she unwinds in her whirlpool bath or warms herself in the sauna. Her existance revolves around water, and the bathroom is the core of her life. Even when she rides her stationary bicycle, she does so with a David Hockney on the wall. This water-oriented lifestyle certainly rewards her with relaxation and consequently health.

The heated swimming pool also serves as a venue for social interaction. The Suzukis entertain many guests, who are always welcome to use the pool. The couple truely desired to create an inviting and enjoyable home and have succeeded remarkably.

As for the bathroom, one wall is a floor-to-ceiling window which provides a bather with a fine view of the outer garden. The bathtub is set a bit above the floor, a touch which hints at the pleasures of an open-air bath.

At any rate, the Japanese love hot springs and open-air bathing. Indulge in an open-air bath and you will feel as if you had become one with nature, a feeling which is decidedly appealing to the Japanese. Of course, this concept of disappearing into nature is Oriental in its origin. Yet it could be argued that while naked in the bath we all feel at home, as though we were some sort of aquatic species. The open-air bath accelerates the process of absorption into nature, and so the Japanese are particularly drawn to this form of bathing.

previous page: The pleasant swimming pool in the Suzuki residence.

right: A bathroom offering a view of an outer garden imparts an open-air feeling.

The Suzuki's home was designed by *Masako Hayashi,*[5] a well-known female architect. The design incorporated the swimming pool, according to the owner's request, and for this reason 734 square meters of building space first had to be found—fairly large by Tokyo standards. The house is L-shaped, with the living area and swimming pool wings meeting at right angles. Between them are located the bathroom, the washstand and the lavatory. The bathroom is at the physical center of the house and, in daily life, surely functions as the core of the house. This is a house in which the lifestyle of the residents and the design of the residence truly complement each other.

(Edogawa, Tokyo)

upper: A washstand area. A sauna room, a bathroom and a lavatory are located on its right. The swimming pool is in the rear.

right: The exterior of the Suzuki's home.

After Gaudi: Echo Timber

This home, which exudes an "urban resort" aura, is a classy residence which was not built to measure for a particular owner but is a unique home constructed according to a design competition. The MCH Research Institute For Living Space held a competition and this *Ushida Findlay Partnership*[6] design was the winner; the firm then built the house. The present owner, who is the proprietor of an art gallery, uses it as his guest house.

Driving through the sprawling Tokyo metropolis to reach a suburban second house on the weekend is an enervating experience. It can take several hours to inch through the relentless traffic jams, and spending holidays this way can leave one feeling even more stressed rather than at ease. Thus it is crucial that a refuge within the city be maintained, as time and space for leisure must be available without the necessity of driving to the suburbs. Such havens within the city are known as urban resorts. Echo Timber was built with the intention of making relaxation and satisfaction available in central Tokyo.

A living room and a dining room, along with a bathroom, occupy the first floor, and there are two bedrooms upstairs. All the rooms on the first floor face an outer garden, and when the large glass doors are opened the living and dining areas expand as they incorporate the garden. The garden itself possesses a hint of a primitive Mexican motif, which is carried into the living and dining rooms as well. Thanks to this decor, the house brims with vital holiday spirit and would make a wonderful venue for a party.

The bathroom is indeed attractive, bringing to mind the mysterious interior of a seashell. It is done in a blue tile mosaic which features undulating lines, imparting an air reminiscent of the Spanish architect Antoni Gaudi. With the bathroom windows open, one's gaze cast over the garden and one's body immersed in the whirlpool bath, it seems that there could be no better holiday experience anywhere. This bathroom is located between and connects with the dining room and the living room, so the architectural center of the structure is the whirlpool. The most luxurious resort mood can be enjoyed in this central bath. The garden which the bathroom faces has a small pool, and those who have become a bit tipsy with champagne and wine are free to wander out of the bathroom toward the poolside and sit down for a chat. All of these concepts are really vacation feeling.

This house seems to encourage a fun-filled lifestyle. The artistic bathroom is the conceptual core of this light-hearted residence. As we've described, water plays a major role in creating an enjoyable lifestyle. The intriguing bathroom space with its blue hues is a prototype of water-related architecture in an environment designed for entertaining. "Aqua Parties" will be one of the most characteristic events creating new social relations in the 1990s.

(Suginami, Tokyo)

upper: Echo Timber as seen from the street.

opposite: The bathroom evokes the mysterious beauty of a seashell and creates an art nouveau impression.

right: The dining room with its movable glass doors. Upon opening the doors the dining and living space are united with the courtyard, creating a fabulous environment for a garden party. The courtyard has a small pond, and the bathroom is to its right.

opposite: The courtyard viewed form the vacation feeling, living room. At the far side are the bathroom window.

On the Seaside of Mediterranean Sea: The Ukita Residence

lower: The glowing white bathroom of the Ukita residence, with the owner obviously enjoying their bath time.

opposite: A bedroom. On Sundays the couple enjoy brunch under the parasol on the balcony.

An exterior view of the Ukita residence.

Films set in Mediterranean surroundings depict the lives of those who spend their days in brilliant sunshine. This was the conceptual inspiration for Mrs. Ukita's bathroom—a white and radiant space. In such an environment, with accents of greenery and vivid colors, we can truly refresh ourselves.

Mr. Ukita rises a bit later than ordinary on Sunday mornings. He takes a rather long sauna bath, then splashes into a bathtub. Next he spends some time in front of a mirror for facial grooming before having a lengthy whirlpool bath. Obviously, he takes his time about bathing. Returning to the bedroom in a bath robe, he retires to the balcony where he ensconces himself below a parasol. There, Mr. and Mrs. Ukita sip a cool glass of beer and nibble on some nuts and a salad. A comfortable life, wouldn't you agree? The period immediately following a nice bath is a glorious time. A pleasant morning and a tranquil bath are not extravagances but rather can enrich anyone's life. The after-bath interval is also important, since this period completes the bathing experience.

Mrs. Ukita's neat white bathroom on the seaside of Mediterranean Sea is a shining emblem of her family's happiness. The hero and heroine of this script, Mr. and Mrs. Ukita, always smile softly as though they were characters in a film.

The design is a joint product of Mrs. Ukita, who is an interior coordinator, and *Minami House Design and Construction Co., Ltd.*[7]

(Setagaya, Tokyo)

What's Going on the Bathrooms of These Major People?

A collection of Yukiko Hanai.

Ms Manami Fuji

Actress *Manami Fuji*[8] is extraordinarily fond of bathing. Her villa on the Izu Penninsula is a three-story structure perched on a cliff overlooking the Pacific Ocean. The bathroom, situated on a projecting corner of the third floor, provides her with a spectacular view of the Izu Seven Islands in the distance. The bathroom is constructed of elegant "Izu stones" and natural hot spring water is plumbed directly to the bath, making for an exceptionally pleasing and comfortable bath time.

The night view is another wonderful aspect of Ms. Fuji's bath. Turning off the lights, the eye wanders over the far-off flickering lights of the cuttlefish fleet. The body melds into the bath as if it were the sea, providing both a physical and mental release.

Ms. Fuji is long-time lover of hot springs. She often visits Yugashima hot spring resort with friends, and comments that her favorite hotel there is the countrified inn where famous novelist Motojiro Kajii once stayed. After a long bath, she favors sipping sake and enjoying the companionship of her friends.

Busy writing books these days, the actress is often asked to appear as a guest on a television program which features haiku groups. She enjoys opera on laser discs in her free time.

Regretfully, Ms. Fuji's busy acting career prevents her from spending as much time at the villa as she would prefer. Although the land was purchased twenty years ago, she built the villa only recently. The private hot spring and the spectacular view are what enticed her to acquire this particular plot, as she has always nursed a dream of owning a luxurious place for her own private bath time. The villa also sports a sauna bath large enough for four. She enjoys sharing the bath and sauna with her family and friends, who return to Tokyo from these visits revitalized in both body and mind. Beyond all doubt, her villa provides a superlative environment for resting, reading and writing.

Moreover, the bathroom at Ms. Fuji's Tokyo residence is also unusually comfortable. The pinkish bath is to be found again on the highest and best floor of the three-story house. Weary from a long day's work, she returns home and begins her bath ritual while watching the highlights of the day's pro baseball activity on a large-screen TV. Then, opening the shades of the skylight, she settles in for an hour-long bath. During this time she occasionally strolls out to a mirrored room for hair and facial grooming, after which she again eases back into the bath. Such a star-lit bath is indeed romantic. All things which enrich body and mind are appealing to Manami Fuji, so she loves to eat, drink and bathe. Her philosophy of life is that a comfortable body and mind lead to beauty.

(Izu Shizuoka Prefecture, and Shinjuku, Tokyo)

Ms Manami Fuji

upper: A bathroom in Ms Fuji's Tokyo residence. Its pinkish shades make it undeniably gorgeous in the midnight.

lower left: A photograph of the Izu villa.

lower right: A bathroom plumbed to a private hot spring. The spectacular view of the Izu Seven Islands is overwhelming. (Photos: the Third Space)

Yukiko Hanai

opposite: A bathroom in Yukiko Hanai's villa. High quality hot-spring water is piped in for her private use, and with it, the luxurious feeling of open-air bathing becomes accessible.

lower: The bathroom viewed from the powder room. With the windows opened, its magnificent and sophisticated design is indeed impressive.

Yukiko Hanai[9] is one of the leading figures in Japan's world of fashion design. Her dresses, with their exquisite feminine lines, are unfailingly glamorous. Japanese women love dresses by Yukiko Hanai and their flowerlike beauty.

The designer's villa at Hakone is well-known for the unique and elaborate design of its bathroom. Interestingly enough, it has somewhat of a masculine aura about it—quite a contrast to her dresses. The architect *Eizo Shiina*[10] is responsible for this design which impressively blends tenderness and strength. Employing wood and stone as building materials, he expressed the artistry of traditional Japanese architecture in this thoroughly original design. Because the windows slide entirely into the walls when opened a grand communion with nature at large can be experienced with the removal of all obstacles from before the eye. This dynamic feeling actually does arise when we occupy an open space overlooking a magnificent landscape.

The bathroom design is certainly sophisticated, with black a key color. The black granite construction produces an ultra-modern luster. A stylish powder room, done in black and gold, features a shell collection neatly arranged on the cabinet.

upper: 1991 spring and summer offering from Yukiko Hanai. Her garments are acclaimed for their delicate feminine lines.

right: Yukiko Hanai.

left: The living room of Yukiko Hanai's villa.

right: Another view of the living room. The large pillars create an impression of tenderness mingled with strength.

With the windows slid into the walls, the sight of the pine trees outside overwhelms one with the presence of the natural world. In the mirror the bathtub filled with milky-white natural hot spring water beckons us with its gently rising vapors.

Opening the large glass door and entering the bathroom, the black granite tub, which comfortably accommodates three, is a welcoming sight. Top-quality natural thermal water is piped in for our use and a healthy bath may be enjoyed whenever one pleases. With the windows opened into the walls, we are soon transported to the dreamy world of the open-air bath. The design has captured the essence of the wild outdoors and mated it to the comforts of an indoor spa. In this gorgeous bathing space the Hanais can enjoy a more luxurious bath time at home than is offered at a commercial spa.

What a fantastic bath it is! Most likely, this is the bath all Japanese wish they could call their own.

This villa is the Hanai's favorite place to spend their time. They visit often, on holidays and during their summer vacation, and invite friends and artists from her fashion circle to join them there. She never misses a chance to urge her guests to enjoy the pleasures offered by this wonderful bath. Without a doubt both her fashions and her bath make people feel happy and gorgeous.

(Hakone, Kanagawa Prefecture)

The Author's Bath
Art Deco Drama: Akira Tsumura

opposite: A dynamic bathroom accentuated by flowing hot water.

right: A bathroom with a whirlpool.

The same bathroom; with a powder room is in the right rear, a water bath on the left, and a shower room and sauna in the left rear. The outstanding design features marble walls and golden tile and pillars. A TV set is installed in the wall opposite.

Splendid decorations accent the bathrooms of Akira Tsumura, author of the present volume. His home in the fashionable Shibuya district of central Tokyo is so filled with artworks from his extensive collection as to resemble a museum. Its unique architectural qualities and art deco style never fail to leave visitors with a strong impression.

There is marble in a variety of shades—pink, green and red—with golden decorations here and there enhancing the effect. The frescos contribute to the distinguished image this residence projects. The many ornaments with animal themes contribute a dramatic touch of the baroque.

As for its bathrooms, this home features baths attached to each of its rooms. The third-floor bath is particularly large and well-designed. Passing through the pink marble powder room, we enter the spacious bathroom itself. To the right is a whirlpool bath and on the left a conventional bathtub. Beyond lies a shower room and still further is a sauna bath. All the walls are of green marble, the ceiling blue tile, and the floor is done in stone and golden tile. The pillars glow golden. A skylight features illuminated stained glass. Bird and animal ornaments fill nearly all available space. All these elements work together to create a dramatic air in these rooms. The bath seems as though inspired by music video: it is a space of the imagination.

Video displays are located in the sauna and the bathroom, so the author can enjoy a leisurely bath while watching. The house also contains a private gym which allows Tsumura to train while appreciating the artworks hung on the walls. The source of the vitality which powers his energetic life is here in this dynamic space which brings together athletic conditioning, whirlpool, sauna and bath.

upper: The same bathroom with a water bath.

lower: The objet d'art TV installation which is surrounded by decorated shells.

41

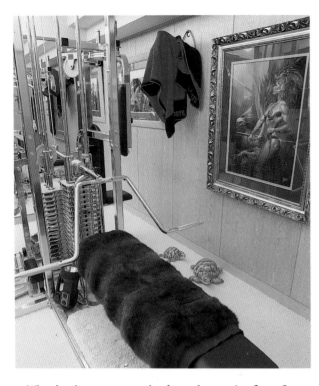

left: The gym.

right: The inside of a sauna. While taking a leisurely bath, the owner can watch video.

lower right and opposite: The bathroom attached to the main bedroom on the first floor.

The bathroom attached to the main first-floor bedroom is exquisitely decorated in art deco black and silver. Though it resembles the bathroom of the Hotel Morgan (the work of noted designer Andree Putman), it produces an impression of even greater substance and supruousness. A refined and well-designed bathroom such as this is un-questionably a form of epicureanism for lovers of the bath.

The courtyard plays an important role in the aqueous environment of this home. Its stone pros-pect is visible from the second-floor dining room. Water slides down the outer wall of the entrance hall before plunging vertically into the courtyard, and after flowing around the perimeter of the courtyard it finally enters the house. As dusk fades into night, the author enjoys dinner while taking in the remote-controlled television display on the opposite side of the dining room. The large-screen TV has been installed in an objet d'art inspired by the Empire State Building. This is indeed a scene from a science fiction movie.

(Shibuya, Tokyo)

opposite: The dining room, which almost seems to have materialized from an SF movie. Under the television, water runs in a miniature waterfall.

left: The courtyard. Water slides down the front wall, crosses the courtyard, and enters the house.

How do Foreigners Enjoy Japanesque Bath Life?

Many longtime foreign residents of Japan have found themselves becoming aficionados of the bath. Taking pleasure in various styles of bathing, most like hot springs and in many cases know how to enjoy them better than the Japanese. Thus, we will next take a look at the Japanesque bath life of some foreign residents.

Dr. Precker's room seen from an entrance (to the right) of the Wilk and Precker residence.

An Old-Fashioned Japanese Bath: Mr. Wilk and Dr. Precker

left: A dining room with blue walls and antique furniture, which combine to create a stylish appearance. The door in the left foreground was brought from Indonesia.

opposite: The bathroom with a Japanese lantern visible in the garden. It recalls the mood of a forgotten Japan.

upper: The living room.

lower: The front entrance.

opposite: An exterior view of Mr. Wilk and Dr. Preckers's home.

In a sense, Mr. Wilk and Dr. Precker enjoy life in Japan more than ordinary Japanese do. They have lived in Japan and Southeast Asia for twenty three years, and possess a thorough understanding of Japanese culture. The two have created a home which blends Occidental and Oriental influences and expresses their world-view.

The house was originally built for a famous individual and was designed by wellknown architect *Yoshinobu Ashihara*[11] thirty-some years ago in the split-level style of the American architect Breuer. After purchasing the residence Mr. Wilk and Dr. Precker remodeled it into its present configuration. One example of the changes wrought is the transformation of a small maid's room into an unusual dining space featuring blue walls and *shoji* (sliding paper screens). The former ceiling was peeled off, the walls redesigned and an Indonesian open-work door installed, and the old maid's room was reborn as an entirely different space.

Quantities of artwork collected over many years fill the living room and the study—European and Oriental antiques and Japanese works of art—which produces an intriguing air approaching that of a sort of residential antique museum. In these surroundings each and every piece is given a new life; there are thirteen such rooms in the house. Mr. Wilk and Dr. Precker have remodeled each of these rooms, making use of their elaborate skills and imaginations, and no room is a repetition of any other. Each room reveals something different about the lives of the owners.

These two Americans appreciate the traditional Japanese lifestyle more than typical Japanese do. Eschewing Western beds, they have long been sleeping on Japanese *futon* in a *tatami* room.

Their antique bathroom also differs from the very convenient kind now popular in Japan, but they treasure it and make use of it daily. While it might appear outdated to contemporary Japanese, who are so accustomed to modern bathrooms, it cannot be denied that this traditional bath with its stone tub, oak cover and Japanese lantern evokes a forgotten aura of ancient Japan. Needless to say,

the pair are much enamored of the traditional aesthetics of Japan, and integrate these concepts into their everyday lives with a passion.

They follow the Japanese procedure when bathing, of course. After warming in the tub, they wash outside and again sink into the hot water to completely warm and relax themselves. Many foreign residents of Japan enthusiastically point out that this bathing technique is beneficial for the health because it thoroughly releases tension from the body and increases the effectiveness of the bath.

(Tokyo)

A Bathroom Like a Movie Set: Agnes Guibout

Agnes Guibout, a French fashion director, is another foreigner who is imbued with a profound understanding of the Japanese philosophy of beauty. Though an excessive emphasis on the Japanesque can of course be in nothing but bad taste, this lady's sophisticated fashion sense makes her interior design efforts wonderfully chic.

If anything, Japanese yearn for Western culture and tend to favor Westernstyle housing. However, at the same time, Westerners fantasize about the Orient. Those foreigners who love Japan generally love it for its traditional aesthetic sensibility, and indeed there are cases in which they love Japan more than the natives do. It follows that foreigners living in Japan inevitably find their tastes shifting toward the Japanesque at some point, but Ms. Agnes Guibout is an exception in this regard. Her taste regarding the Japanesque is sophisticated enough that she can successfully harmonize both French and Japanese styles. Her home is a fantastic, dreamy place which would not be out of place on a movie set.

In decorating the dining room she has made effective use of the Japanese *kimono* and its *obi*, or sash, and produced an effect of delicate prettiness. The bedroom is done in light purple. The interior design as a whole is quite attractive due to the satisfying blend of her fashion sense and her flair for making use of things Japanese. The bathroom is an indescribable space which boldly combines black, white and red. A red French curtain creates an accent, while the large black bathtub draws the eye as the focal point. This cool and intelligent atmosphere is, in a word, impressive.

In the evening, she enjoys long candle-lit baths. The ritual frees her imagination and fires her creativity. Her bath symbolizes the best and most private part of her personal vision.

(Shimada, Shizuoka Prefecture)

A bathroom.

upper: The dining room glimpsed from the living room.

opposite: A bedroom of Agnes Guibout's home.

Communication in the Whirlpool

Whirlpool[12] baths are increasingly popular in Japan these days. Growing numbers of people are enjoying these baths with their families and friends while wearing swimsuits. Even Japanese who love the fellowship of the bath lack the nerve to bathe naked with their friends and family members, but once they don a swimsuit everything is fine. In fact, today's younger generation is not interested in the nude communal bathing around which local communication networks once formed.

Nowadays, some people have private whirlpool baths large enough to hold several bathers in comfort, which provide a place where they can enjoy an easy flow of conversation among friends and relatives.

Whirlpool Party: The Kanazawa Residence

The Shimoda resort area is located at the very tip of the Izu Peninsula and thus is favored with a mild climate even in winter. Mrs. Kanazawa's home in Shimoda stands just beside the sea, offering a fine view of the waves rolling in. The likeness of this house, with its white arches, is commonly seen in California. The sea is visible from every room of the structure, while a broad yard surrounds the house. Just imagine having a cup of afternoon tea, seated in a simple white chair and surrounded by roses in the warm spring breeze. It sounds terrific, doesn't it?

The owner was formerly a confirmed city resident, and spent quite a while living in the exciting Roppongi district smack in central Tokyo. She built the Shimoda house so that she could pass her retirement years in a mild climate. Since lifespans are growing longer these days, the issue of how to spend one's older years is becoming topical. The splendid lifestyle which Mrs. Kanazawa is able to enjoy today is proof that she has made good choices throughout her life. She maintains her condominium in Tokyo and enjoys visiting the city once or twice a month. It's a comfortable life for her, alternating in turn between her two residences.

Shimoda and Tokyo are separated by a mere two-hour train journey, and because of this convenience the town serves as a resort area for Tokyo residents. Yet since Mrs. Kanazawa lives in Shimoda and only occasionally spends time in Tokyo, the urban residence could more properly be called a vacation home in her case.

Mrs. Kanazawa's daughter is constantly sending her interior and gardening magazines from California, which serve as a steady source of inspiration and guidance for home decoration. Mrs. Kanazawa enjoys keeping busy—taking care of plants, acquiring new housewares, and doing many other household chores. Even when purchasing something as minor as a new plant she is sensitive to the

The living room of the Kanazawa residence.

The hot spring whirlpool in the courtyard.

needs of her grandchildren, always doing her best to prepare the house for them. Her tender heart is evident in a variety of touches all around the house.

There are three guest rooms, each with its own bathroom of course. This is no exception in contemporary Japan, where housing styles have shifted drastically to Western models. It was long a custom that a family share the bathroom, but this is becoming passe these days. While it must be admitted that there are still small houses which lack sufficient space for bathrooms attached to each bedroom, Mrs. Kanazawa faces no such problem.

Surrounded by arches, the courtyard sports a whirlpool bath large enough to accomodate four or five in comfort, and hot spring water is piped in to feed the bath. This hot-spring whirlpool stimulates health and beauty, and is popular with the children as well. The grandchildren always visit in summer with their parents and the whirlpool is then crowded with the youngsters. After swimming at the nearby private beach people all jump into the whirlpool, and quench their thirst at the counter bar in the courtyard. It's time for a whirlpool party! Aqua Party! The grandchildren make merry in the whirlpool, having a terrific time. Then, tired of playing, they retire to their rooms to bathe and wash off the sand. Throwing themselves over the beds, they gaze out over the wide blue sea—truely a refreshing experience, don't you agree?

Mrs. Kanazawa built this house in order to enjoy her life to the greatest extent possible. The whirlpool is the core element of the total architectural concept. It is said that the trend of the 1990s will be toward the family, and if so one of the most trendy pastimes of the decade could well be the family party in the whirlpool bath. This kind of party brings us back to nature and deepens communication among family members. As Mrs. Kanazawa's residence demonstrates, the bath can provide the best of leisure together with a touch of luxury.

(Shimoda, Shizuoka Prefecture)

upper: A guest room beyond the bar in the courtyard.

lower: An exterior view of the Kanazawa residence. (Photo: Koji Horiuchi)

The Relaxing Life Style of a Home Worker: Naozo Sugimoto

When the weather is clear the deep blue sky glows far above the graceful white birches. The air is clean and fresh. This, in every respect, is a Swiss paradise in Japan. It was many years ago that Mr. Sugimoto, formerly a television director, found his way here. One of those who have abandoned city life, he now lives a life closer to nature in his log house.

The Japanese have given up much for city life—health, purity and family ties have been among the sacrifices. They are disgusted with the extent to which they have been victimized by their losses. However, today it is possible to work even while living far out in the country since information services link rural and urban areas and transportation facilities have made it easy to travel from country to city. Thus the"back to the country" movement has been gathering momentum in recent years.

Mr. Sugimoto works at home, his office in the most comfortable room of his log house, elegantly handling his chores with the aid of computer and facsimile machine. His residence in Suwa is within a two-hour drive of Tokyo by expressway, and he often comes to the city to meet with colleagues and customers. Anyone could envy his relaxed lifestyle of working at his own home. He solemnly declares that his motto is "Never work to excess."

From his home, which has been beautifully decorated to serve as a showpiece, he engages in the business of building log houses, and has been responsible for constructing over 40 log structures, including restaurants and hotels, over the past four years alone. All his buildings are made of genuine fir logs imported from the northern United States. When he recommends a log house to a customer he at the same time is proposing an "ecology life": this is what people are longing for and what only a log house can make possible. Mr. Sugimoto has lived his "ecology life" for over ten

The whirlpool outside the Sugimoto residence, along with the sauna, against the backdrop of a stand of larch trees.

years. His life, lived in harmony with nature, is a message to this age.

The foundation of Mr. Sugimoto's natural lifestyle is the tranquility which he enjoys while taking a bath. His home has three baths, and in addition a whirlpool bath and a barrel sauna are located in the garden. He often gathers his friends for outdoor wine parties, and since they can warm themselves in the sauna these parties are held even in the winter snow. The natural setting leads to heart-to-heart communication among the participants.

"Workaholism" is no longer being cheered in Japan. We should now pursue a more stress-free lifestyle, pay more attention to our health, and live in harmony with the natural world. As the first step toward meeting these goals, what could be more appropriate than a satisfying bathing experience?

(Suwa, Nagano Prefecture)

left: The first floor bathroom.

upper: The second floor bathroom. Its natural atmosphere commands the visitor's attention.

62

Bath Time for Ecologists: Pension Alm

Located at the foot of spectacular Mount Yatsugatake near the Japan Alps, a setting reminiscent more of Switzerland than Japan, *Pension Alm*[13] occupies a log structure. Its owner, who loves the mountains above all else, built the small inn to accommodate his post-retirement life. He used to live in the city, but tired of it and returned to the country. Now he has a real "ecology life." The coziness of this highland retreat brings to mind the pleasures of a simple mountain hut.

Two major attractions of this pension are its large whirlpool, and the barrel baths, which were imported directly from Canada. One can enjoy a honestly natural bath time while immersed in the spacious tub in the quiet mountain atmosphere: it takes but a moment to forget the complications of urban life. White birches, seen through the skylight, appear to be scraping the deep blue sky—a sight to open the senses. The primitive gentleness of the rough-hewn logs and the subtle beauty of

Pension Alm. In the distance on the far right lies the Yatsugatake chain of mountains.

The large barrel bathtub of Pension Alm.

the barrel wall penetrate deeply into one's heart. This is a bath experience which profoundly refreshes the heart. In modern life, with all its tensions and anxieties, what is good for the body is good for the spirit. Physical welfare is now being pursued eagerly by an urban populace which finds it difficult to maintain health in today's world. Certainly it is practically impossible to be sound in spirit without being attuned to the Earth for the good of future genertions.

(Tateshina, Nagano Prefecture)

A dining room.

Bath Resorts

Since ancient days, a profound love of bathing has driven the Japanese to incorporate bathing within the resort experience and has motivated them to seek out and visit natural hot springs. Public baths, serving as "neighborhood resorts," have also enriched the lives of the common folk. Today, the bathing resorts which have for so long been developed and patronized by the Japanese are at a turning point beyond which they will present different qualities from those which were ordinary in the past.

Japan's resorts are now being obligated to rejuvinate themselves by applying new concepts which package leisure, sports, meals and accommodation facilities. Even in the face of such sweeping changes, the first priority set by this land's born bathers is the upgrading of bathing facilities. Hotels and inns are concentrating their efforts on innovative interior design and the introduction of healthy amenities in order to project with force an image of renewal, and consequently spa resorts are enjoying unprecedented popularity. Sports clubs and country clubs are also offering whirlpools, saunas and other varieties of baths to take advantage of the benefits which bathing bestows upon their clientele. It shouldn't be forgotten that the bath can provide an ideal environment for social intercourse for the Japanese people, who without exception like to bathe in the company of friends and relatives.

Thus baths are playing an important role in resort life. There is as well an increasing interest in utilizing spas to improve the health. One facility designed for this purpose is the *kurhaus*.[14] Beyond relaxation, the bath is being used more and more actively as a means to build a good health. This phenomenon is drawing increasing attention. In any event, it can well be concluded that bathing is the greatest attraction which resorts hold for the Japanese.

The heated swimming pool at Southern Cross Resort.

The New Wave Country Club: Southern Cross Resort

An outdoor hot-spring whirlpool bath. A golf course is visible in the distance.

Southern Cross Resort[15] is transforming itself into a new type of golf-centered resort complex. Located on the Izu Peninsula, a golf course was built here in the 1950's and a hotel completed in the 1970's. A swimming pool, restaurants and shops were added in the late 1980's.

Golf is quite popular these days among young women. When asked where they would most like to play, Southern Cross Resort is the unanimous choice. This country club is new in every respect with its new concepts and new facilities. The club often advertises package holidays in women's magazines: a round of golf on the short course, tennis, swimming, meals and a night's accommodation all for $200 per person—an attractive and economical offering which tempts even veteran players.

A young Japanese woman is generally in search of a good boyfriend who has a car and likes tennis and skiing. Though there are some who are ambitious enough to disregard a young man unless he drives a BMW and earns over $100,000 a year, most ordinary young females are basically seeking a partner with whom they can spend their time enjoyably.

Such a couple might leave Tokyo for Izu by car on a Saturday morning, checking in at the club at around one o'clock in the afternoon. After changing clothes, they play tennis and take a dip in the heated pool, later finding themselves settled into the hot spring whirlpool for a quiet chat while admiring the grandeur of the sunset over the Izu Peninsula. Having had a nice talk in the bath and feeling both physically and spiritually refreshed, they retire to their room for a shower. Then, donning brand-new casual outfits, they stroll to the restaurant for an eagerly anticipated repast.

Early the following day they play a round on the short golf course. While not particularly skillful players, they don't let this bother them since they pursue the game as a means of relaxation rather than as a competitive sport— enjoying the game is their purpose. Finally, they drive back to the city on Sunday afternoon.

A restaurant interior view.

Whirlpools, which can be enjoyed in a bathing suit, appeal to this sort of young couple. The truth is they don't like bathing nude with friends or family members, much less with absolute strangers at conventional spas. More and more ski resorts and hotels offer whirlpools these days, since such young people are fond of partaking of these baths in the same way in which they enjoy sport. Southern Cross Resort boasts a hot-spring whirlpool which pleasantly warms bathers and relieves the fatigue brought on by playing sports.

(Ito, Shizuoka Prefecture)

Kurhaus: Mer Club

The *kurhaus* is a facility which promotes health by making use of natural hot spring waters. Japan is among those countries in which bathing in thermal spring water is extremely popular. Moreover, a heightened health consciousness has in recent years increasingly prevailed not only among those of middle and advanced ages but among the young as well. People strongly desire lifestyles which are healthy and more vital. In these circumstances, *kurhaus* facilities are increasingly in demand. Hot spring bathing has the psychotheraputic effect of washing away the "techno-stress" which accumulates among members of an information-intensive society. It adjusts the performance of the nervous system's autonomous functions and various other biological processes, and relieves stress and muscular fatigue. It can also cure diabetes, rheumatism and high blood pressure. In a word, the hot

upper: A neighbor enjoying a dip in one of MER CLUB's hot spring pool.

lower: The hot-spring swimming pool.

spring provides the best means of overhauling the body and the spirit. For these reasons, the demand for *kurhaus* facilities will continue to grow in the future.

The theme for the 1990's of the Japanese people is how to rest and live a stress-free life. Under these circumstances, the "science of repose" is now a popular topic. To make use of the *kurhaus,* the best means of attaining good health, is to incorporate this "science" in one's life.

Mer Club,[16] situated on the Izu Peninsula in Shimoda, is owned by a sports doctor and now is implementing a health promotion program founded on the use of thermal spring waters and centering on sports activities. Equipped with a 25 meter swimming pool, it offers swimming classes for mothers and children. The owner's desire to employ the hot spring in improving client's health is gradually becoming a reality. Neighborhood residents often swim in the hot-spring pool; anyone can use this facility for a reasonable membership fee and usage charge.

The club also features a gym, and basic medical instruments for health evaluation are on hand. Visitors can not only enjoy the effects of hot-spring bathing but can also maintain their physical fitness here. Next to the swimming pool are a powerful whirlpool, an *utase-yu*[17] (artificial waterfall for a shower-massage effect) and a *ne-yu*[18] (shallow bath in which bathers may recline).

The *kurhaus,* brimming with a healthy and sporty appeal, is particularly popular among young people nowadays, since it frees them from the embarrassment of nudity they experience at conventional hot springs. They can enjoy bathing as a sort of healthy sport.

(Izu, Shizuoka Prefecture)

upper: Guests relaxing in a hot-spring whirlpool.

lower: The hot-spring whirlpool along with the *ne-yu* (a shallow pool of tepid water) to the rear and the *utase-yu* (an artificial waterfall where warm water drops on a bather's shoulders) on the left. A private hot spring is the source of these baths' medicinal value.

A Trendy Sports Club: Spatz

The Shibuya district is an important sub-center within central Tokyo. *Spatz,*[19] a sports club which opened there in 1990, is, in a sense, a symbol of the affluence of present-day Japan. Its nine stories above-ground and two below house a comprehensive athletic club which is most welcome by connoisseurs of the urban resort.

Weekday mornings, executives from various firms swim in the 25 meter pool before work. The gym, with its staff of first-rank instructors, is like a scene from a music video. The aerobics studio is always crowded with well-to-do housewives. A driving range offers golf lessons, and squash courts are available as well. At the diving pool, 5.5 meters deep, scuba diving is taught. Lounges and party rooms for member's use are located on the seventh and eighth floors.

Enjoy city life at Spatz—spend some time reading a book or tanning on the sixth-floor sun deck overlooking the bustling streets below. When you get too warm, dip into the open whirlpool.

One of the most distinctive characteristics of this club is the variety of baths available: various types of whirlpools, an *utase-yu,* a sauna, a cold-water bath, and a mistsauna, which features the invigorating aroma of mountain herbs.

Relieve your stress and relax and refresh yourself in these baths. Spatz is a trendy club which appeals to those busy executives who tend to work too much and are chronically tired.

(Shibuya, Tokyo)

upper left: An exterior view of Spatz.

upper right: An entrance. The blue area opposite is a diving pool.

lower: The 25-meter swimming pool on the second floor. To the right in the rear is a whirlpool.

upper left: The sun deck on the sixth floor. This is a fine place for getting a nice suntan. A large whirlpool is located here as well.

upper right: A resort-style pool on the sixth floor. It is designed not for swimming but rather for relaxation by playing in the water.

lower leftt: Restaurant Sera on the first floor. On the walls hang Liechtenstein prints.

lower right: There are seven different baths in the first basement—a whirlpool, a utase-yu, a mistsauna, a dry sauna, a water bath and so on.

right: Mistsauna.

extreme right: Utase-yu.

(Photos: the Third Space)

Andree Putman's Hotel: Le Lac

Andree Putman,[20] a world-famous French interior designer, is often mistaken for a bathroom designer because of her unparalleled enthusiasm for bathroom design. The list of her accomplishments includes New York City's Morgan Hotel, President Mitterand's library, boutiques for *Yve Saint Laurent* and *Thierry Mugler,* the Contemporary Art Museum in Bordeau, and the VIP room used for the Paris summit conference. Her designs, which are thoroughly up-to-date, are based on a serene aesthetic.

Her first work in Japan is the small hotel known as *Le Lac*[21] on the shore of Lake Kawaguchi. With its eight guest rooms, housed in a remodelled inn, it offers visitors a quiet and intimate refuge.

Le Lac is a little more than an hour from central Tokyo by car. Our first impression is provoked by the severe copper entrance door, which conjures associations with Bauhaus. No less striking is the beautiful entrance hall with its straight-forward lighting. The guest rooms on the second floor have been done in earth tones, while blue shades predominate in those on the third floor. The rooms feature spacious baths placed immediately before the large beds, with the landscape visible through a window beyond.

This hotel is best enjoyed by couples. The man might stretch out on the bed with a glass of fine wine provided by room service, while his companion busies herself in the bath. If shy she might close the folding door, which presents him with an even more tantalizing image through the translucent glass. This is a bathroom that reflects sensibilities typical of the passionate French .

The bathroom has a cute washbasin of blue tile, a shower to the left and a tiled bathtub to the right. The lady might chat from the bath with her man, who reclines on the bed sipping wine and watching television, about tomorrow's round of golf, the opera she attended last week, or perhaps a new dress she picked up recently. When she emerges after her bath wrapped in a white bath robe, he will already have drifted off to sleep with the aid of the wine. Good wine is as soothing to the entire body as a good bath.

This is a bathroom drama that no-one but Putman could write. She is the world's leading bathroom designer.

The hotel's restaurant serves Italian cuisine. The dishes served up by the first-rate chef, together with the beautiful interior, set the stage for fantastic nights at this romantic lakeside retreat.

opposite: A bathroom at Le Lac.
overleaf left: A living area.
overleaf right: The entrance hall.

Japan's Finest Hot Spring Inn: Yagyu No Sho

Perched at the very top of its class, the celebrated *Yagyu No Sho*[22] was designed by an acknowledged authority on Japanese architecture, *Okada Architectural Office*.[23] As would be expected, it is a superlative interpretation of Japanese aesthetics. Its relatively few rooms are almost always fully booked, and more than a few people harbor a wish to reserve a room and enjoy a stay at least once in their lifetimes. The owner formerly operated a Japanese-style restaurant in Tokyo, and chose the noted moon-viewing site of Shuzenji when planning for the inn. A splendid open-air bath, exquisite Japanese-style rooms, a gourmet menu, impeccable service: all come together here to distinguish Yagyu No Sho as champion among the hot spring inns of Japan.

Standing in the midst of a bamboo thicket, the inn delivers wonderful views of the seasonal changes in its garden. Each room is elaborately decorated in one of three traditional Japanese styles—tea house, farmhouse, and *shoin*[24] (feudal). Furthermore, the inn itself was tastefully designed in the 16th century *sukiya*[25] style and constructed entirely of Japanese cypress. All the guest rooms are as though detached from the main structure, ensuring that guests are able to relax themselves completely. In addition, open-air baths are attached to each guest room. A better inn is not to be found.

Bathing is not the exclusive concern at Japan's hot spring resorts, which provide for all elements of leisure which Japanese tend to seek. Of course an excellent thermal spring is indispensable for a great spa, but beyond this it is necessary that delicious cuisine, quality architecture and excellent service also be present before an inn can be called first-class.

Simply staying at such a place, one feels, must be enough to extend one's life. This may be attributed not only to the repose which rewards hot spring bathers but to all the wonderful details

upper: The entrance of Yagyu No Sho.

lower: Covered passage leading to guest room.

78

which the Japanese have taken into consideration in order to create the ultimate leisure experience.

The large open-air bath in the bamboo thicket warms both body and soul. This sort of handsome open-air bath set enticingly into its natural surroundings is the bath most cherished by the Japanese. An open-air bath of attractive appearance which provides the opportunity to enjoy bathing in unity with nature—here the Japanese find the wellspring of the bathing experience.

(Shuzenji, Shizuoka Prefecture)

An open-air bath enveloped in natural beauty.

left: A garden viewed from the entrance of a guest room.

opposite, upper left: A garden wash basin.

opposite, upper right: The elegant guest rooms are done in a purely Japanese style and are distanced from one another.

opposite, lower left: An interior view of a guest room.

opposite, lower right: A guestroom garden displays the splendor of autumn's reds and yellows.

upper: An offering from the kitchens of Yagyu No Sho.

lower: Other dishes brimming with seasonal appeal.

82

One of Tsumura's series of packaged bath powders of best Japanese hot-springs. These bath powders make hot-spring bathing available even at home.

A Renowned Spa in a Natural Setting: Taiseikan

Autumn is the most beautiful season in Japan. When the mountains are covered with scarlet-tinged leaves and *matsutake* mushrooms favor the table with their scent, the Japanese again desire to draw close to the natural world. Autumn, which brings the Mildwest weather of the year, is the best season for leisure pursuits. People go off to the mountains to enjoy views of the autumn foliage, and make pilgrimages to hot springs with family or friends. Luxurious hotels are undoubtably pleasant, but a hot spring resort in undisturbed natural surroundings is the best match for this most gorgeous season of the year.

Taiseikan[26] rests in a narrow valley far from the workaday world, and is steeped in an atmosphere of long-ago travels. The inn has a long history and has been one of the top hot spring resorts of Hakone since the Edo period before Japan's modernization. It occupies the floor of the Hayakawa Ravine, a hundred-meter drop from the surrounding terrain. Guests are carried down into the ravine to the hotel by privately-operated cable cars. In autumn, the scene is a riot of vivid colors.

The greatest attraction of this inn for most people is, needless to say, its fine open-air bath in this spectacular natural setting. The clear stream flowing through the ravine and the open-air bath with its breath-taking view of the mountains are just what the Japanese picture when they imagine

a spa resort. An authentic open-air bath in natural surroundings must feature quality hot water in which one can warm oneself to the marrow even outdoors. Couples, friends and families all indulge in open-air bathing to the fullness of their hearts to absorb the abundant energy of nature. This custom of bathing out-of-doors arises from the sensible Japanese appreciation of both the bath and the natural world. The origin of the Japanese passion for bathing must lie in this kind of hot spring experience.

(Hakone, Kanagawa Prefecture)

left: Taiseikan and a neighboring hotel.

upper right: The ravine in front of Taiseikan bursting with autumn's red foliage.

lower right: A meal.

An open-air bath at Taiseikan. Its location just beside the rushing stream provides for a wonderfully natural environment.

Body Care and Bath Fashion

Among the new shops constantly opening in Paris and Tokyo, a few specializing in body care or bath fashions are always to be found. These shops are currently enjoying a kind of vogue.

Body shampoos, bath oils, bath powders, body brushes, herbs and potpourri made of natural materials crowd their shelves, and these shops carry a fresh healthy scent. Although these are minor items since people are thinking more about the environment these days they are choosing natural products when they are available. These amenities are symbols of the search for a natural life which characterizes our times.

88

Futuristic Beauty: Shu Uemura Esthetic Salon

Esthetic salons which specialize in body and facial care attract people to the same extent fashion does. The growing interest in the bath is connected with the body care boom.

Caring for the body to produce healthy good looks—this is the fundamental attitude of the 21st century regarding beauty. Today a healthy body is a prerequisite to being an attractive person.

It is a well-known fact that, compared to showering, bathing is better for the body as it promotes metabolic changes and the secretion of particular hormones. The bath is indispensable to healthy good looks. The *Shu Uemura Esthetic Salon*[27] employs the ceramic sand bath and special whirlpool bath to achieve total beauty care.

Shu Uemura, owner of "new-wave" cosmetic boutiques located around the world, opened this salon in 1990 in Tokyo's Omotesando district. The salon's policies are said to be as follows: impart pleasant feelings and a sense of contentment as well as make the skin clear and healthy, and provide continuous access to beauty through mental and physical relaxation. Therefore the salon focuses its attention on stress and changes in the natural environment. The introduction of the two types of baths mentioned above aims at reinforcing the body-care regimen to offer high-grade total care. The immediate reaction of both mind and body to these baths is acknowledged to provide the subject with a profound sense of tranquility, thus contributing to the benefits wrought by esthetic efforts.

To prepare the ceramic sand bath, natural ores are processed into ceramic grains. This sand is heated to approximately 40 degrees centigrade and the entire body is buried in the ceramic sand for 15 to 20 minutes. The electromagnetic waves emitted by the ceramic granules heat the body from within to promote metabolic changes which make the skin clear. Shu Uemura was the first in the esthetic industry to use the ceramic sand bath.

The powerful whirlpool bath, with its 88 nozzles, enhances blood circulation and thus makes the skin smooth, fresh and glowing with health. It is also effective in relieving muscular fatigue and stress. Furthermore, when used jointly with thalassotherapy (treatments employing seawater and sea plants), it functions to reduce body fat.

Making use of these advanced techniques, Shu Uemura Esthetic Salon aims at creating sophisticated and futuristic beauty. Here again, the bath plays a vital role in esthetic enhancement.

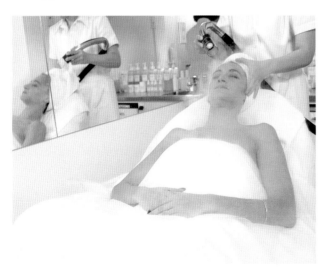

left: Cryocosmetology in action. Using air cooled to −150°C, it effectively removes blemishes, pimples and wrinkles. It can also rejuvenate the body and remove fat.

right: A ceramic sand bath effective in promoting smooth skin.

For a Beautiful Bath: The Body & Bath Shop

The most fashionable of shopping experiences consists of seeking out attractive items for the bathroom or bath products which comfort the body. Shops which handle these products have already appeared in Paris and New York, and more are expected to open all over the world.

The Body & Bath Shop is located on the first floor of a high-tech building at Omotesando, Tokyo. It is among the most comely of all those offering bath fashions, and stocks all manner of excellently designed products: bath towels and bath robes by renowned designers such as *Issey Miyake,* body brushes, physical fitness aids, perfume containers and soap dishes.

Many foreign travelers drop in here when in Tokyo. Some purchase minor bath items, while others, such as VIPs who came to Japan on the occasion of the Emperor's enthronement ceremony, make it a point to purchase quantities of various items. It can safely be said that the boutique expands the imagination regarding the bath.

This year, one trend apparent at the shop is "ecology colors" for towels and bath robes. Tokyo sophisticated fashion world has already expanded to embrace bath fashions. The dying and textures of the towels are most pleasing to the eye. Appreciating attractive bath and body products and creating a gorgeous bath is an exciting and sensual treat.

left: The Body & Bath Shop in Omotesando, Harajuku. (Shu Uemura Esthetic is located in the basement.)

opposite: An original bathrobe from The Body & Bath Shop fashionably done in an ecology color.

left: The interior of the Body and Bath Shop is very stylish high-tech design.

lower left: The interior of the shop.

lower center: Attractive towels which feature the shop's original dyed designs.

lower right: Trendy bath accessories.

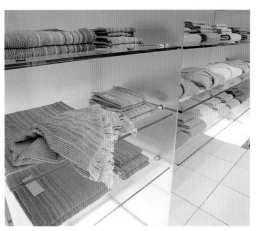

Lovely Bath Accessories

Soaps, brushes, powders and body shampoos—such bath accessories are extremely popular. These amenities for enhancing the bath are becoming increasingly diversified. Shops which specialize in bath potpourri and accessories have opened recently at every department store in Japan. The sight of these goods cheers the heart and gives us the sense of living in a poetic dream.

Some bath products serve not only to increase the pleasures of bathing but also to eliminate stress by luring one into long and leisurely baths. Others, like bath oils and powders, directly fortify the physical efficacy of bathing. All these products augment the bath experience.

Bath oils packaged in the charming shape of marbles within a heart-shaped container are popular as presents among teenagers. They prefer body shampoo to the soap they once used, as they feel that a foamy body shampoo is good for bodycare. If using soap they choose natural unscented products. With their enthusiasm for new bath amenities, trying out a new accessory is enough to make a bath a more enjoyable experience.

Cute bath articles, popular body shampoo and some other goods.
Right, Tsumura's production *PROCESS*.

Various products to enhance the pleasure of one's bath.

upper: A variety of small bath articles for a healthy and relaxing bath.

lower: A popular bath oil.

Designer's Bath Fashions

Recently all manner of bath goods have been introduced by well-known designers in fashion-conscious Japan. Furniture, housewares and personal accessories are beautifully done, and designer brands have not been hesitant to keep pace with the recent explosion of interest in bathing. All designers have marketed bath towels, bath robes and linens in step with the trends of the moment. These products have become popular.

Bath towels and bath robes by *Nicole* are quite elaborate. *Kenzo's* bath items are colorful and pleasing to the eye. Designs by *Yoji Yamamoto* and *Junko Koshino* are also being well-received. *Hanae Mori's* bath fashions are often presented as gifts. Bath towels by *Celine* and *Ralph Lauren* sell well at department stores, along with the products of domestic designers.

Today the youth of Japan has a weakness for merchandise bearing the stamp of a well-known designer. This explains why a young person who happens to own a *Renoma* sofa bed tries to collect an entire set of *Renoma* products, from blankets, towels, and robes to underwear.

In any case, well-designed items for the bath make bath life all the more wonderful and satisfying.

A *Nicolle* bathrobe: the best of everything in terms of material and design.

A gorgeous towel from *Nicolle* featuring golden embroidery.

Bath Powders

With a wide variety of bath powders appearing on the market recently, people are experimenting with one after another to add variety to bathing.

Bath powder not only contributes a pleasant fragrance but acts to heighten the effects of bathing. It facilitates blood circulation and stimulates metabolism, making for a healthier bath. It can safely be said that bath powder is essential to bathing, and the relaxation and comfort which it contributes encourages one to indulge in long and leisurely baths.

It might be a good idea to try a different kind of bath powder with a different fragrance every day. Hot spring bath powders are popular in Japan, as a package bearing the name of a well-known spa inspires the impression that one has had the opportunity to visit that resort without leaving the comforts of home. Regardless, bath powder serves to make bathing more enjoyable and to vanquish stress. This eventually leads to a healthy mind and body and a better life.

upper: A collection of bath powders for a tranquil bath.

lower: Tsumura's series of packaged powders of the best Japanese hot-springs.

The Herbal Bath

Recently bath herbs are becoming increasingly popular, especially among women. Some users create custom fragrances by blending various herbs, since they are not entirely satisfied with the standard offerings of the market. In addition to their excellent fragrance, bath herbs are an effective means of achieving relaxation. One merely places the herbs in a cotton sack and attaches it to the hot water tap—then wait for the bathtub to fill and the bathroom is perfumed with the sweet scent of herbs. An herbal bath is just right for an age in which people are searching for the healthy and the natural.

upper and left: Bath herbs for relaxation. They fill the bathroom with a soft fragrance and make for an elegant bath.

Potpourri

Shops selling potpourri can be found near the entrances of any shopping complex or department store in the most conspicuous location. Potpourri, with its healthy natural scent, is very popular as a "new perfume" for our health-conscious era.

Potpourri, along with life-enhancing housewares, is all the rage today among the young. A variety of country-style goods are usually arranged together with potpourri, and these homey items are selling like mad. Japanese who have become fed up with overly-sophisticated high-tech design trends seem to long for goods which convey a touch of the quiet, peaceful countryside.

People use potpourri so that a room may be scented with its fragrance. Furthermore, they put it in a small sack and slip it into a drawer with underwear. Its natural scent increases the pleasure of one's romantic life.

upper and left: Tsumura Pyxis International Co., Ltd., an exclusive import and wholesale potpourri vendor located in Japan.

Chapter **II**

A HISTORY
OF
THE JAPANESE BATH

Osamu Oba Lecturer of Kyoto Prefectural University

The names of histrical figures are given with the family name preceeding the given name.

Born Bathers

The Japanese people are inordinately fond of bathing. They believe that the best way to relieve the day's fatigue is by immersing themselves in the hot water of the daily bath. The daily bath is, in fact, held to be life's greatest pleasure. Bathing is really one of the most prominent habits that typifies the people of this country.

Why are the Japanese so enthusiastic about bathing? The reasons are very clear. First comes the climate of this island nation, with its extremes of heat and humidity in the summer (excepting Hokkaido, the northernmost island). The all but unbearable muggieness makes people so sweaty and irritated that they cannot do without washing away their perspiration. Everyone, man and woman alike, is well acquainted with the unrivaled feeling of pleasure which follows taking a bath at the end of a steamy summer day.

The volcanic archipelago which makes up Japan is lavishly endowed with hot springs scattered throughout the country, which have been utilized by the inhabitants since ancient times. The Japanese people have enthusiastically patronized these thermal springs for medical and hygienic purposes, not to mention the pleasure of bathing. Ancient records state that even in prehistoric times people spent long periods at *Dogo*[28] and *Arima*[29] spas seeking to cure their ills. This geographical condition, a land studded with hot springs and the towns which have sprung up around them to receive visiting bathers, is an important factor in the background of the Japanese passion for hot water bathing.

Bathing also plays an important role in religious practice. In Shintoism, a religion indigenous to Japan, *misogi* (ritual cleansing) and *harai* (exorcism and purification) are solemn rites performed for self-purification which also have contributed to the prevalence of the practice of bathing. Beyond being merely a means of pleasing or cleansing oneself, bathing is a religious act in the subconsciousness of the people—an embodiment of Japanese culture.

Another reason for the universal inclination to bathing is fear of filth or contamination, which may also be related to religious conceptions. Though it is taken for granted among the Japanese people, their predilection for cleanliness has without exception been a surprise for visitors from abroad. *Basil Hall Chamberlain*[30] spent more than thirty years in Japan from 1873, and compiled his experiences here in his voluminous book "Things Japanese," first published in 1890. He was convinced that the Japanese were the world's cleanest people and that the pursuit of cleanliness was one of few original aspects of their culture.

As grounds for his contention, he cited only the people's fondness for cleanliness, rather than the influence of religious practices such as Shinto. *Chamberlain* concluded that bathing was the most attractive method of maintaining personal cleanliness, which had been demonstrated even by foreigners who were following Japanese practices while in Japan.

This account is only one example. Visitors from other countries in the middle ages and in modern times as well have unanimously and emphatically remarked on the people's adherence to high standards of cleanliness, and have highly praised the cleanliness of the streets where no dirt or dust whatsoever was evident despite the unconcealed shabbiness of the houses.

All told, the Japanese people's penchant for bathing may be attributed to the climate and the geography of the country, and to the religious values and the temperament of this people who pursue cleanliness with a blind passion.

The Steam Bath Tradition

For today's Japanese, taking a bath means soaking oneself in hot water. Though there are some who shower only, most believe that immersion to the chin in *o-yu,* or hot water, is a necessity for overcoming the day's weariness.

It should be noted, however, that the Japanese bath has not remained constant throughout its history. Certainly, bathing styles such as soaking and showering have been popular since ancient times. Hot spring resorts have been developed and patronized as well. In addition, people have routinely bathed in tubs at well- and stream-sides. However, what distinguishes the history of the Japanese bath is in truth the steam bath and its unique methodology.

Regrettably, the traditional steam bath is no longer to be found except in some remote areas. It might be said that something of the original Japanese steam bath still exists, though transformed drastically in its essence, in the popularity of the sauna which was imported from Europe. But these two types of baths are substantially different in their temperatures, and slightly in their atmospheres, in that the medium of the former is steam and of the latter is heated air.

Although few in number and not important in terms of contemporary Japanese bathing habits, the surviving steam baths of Japan are significant when examined in light of the history of the Japanese bath. Along the shores of the Seto Inland Sea, there once were numerous steam baths called *ishi-buro* ("stone baths") which were built in natural caves or in holes drilled in the rock. Villagers lit wood fires inside these bathing holes and removed the ashes after firewood had been consumed, next laying down wall to wall mats which had been soaked in sea water. The heat emanating from the rock surface together with the steam rising from the mats made for an extremely primitive bath that combined the properties of steam and heated-air baths. Bathers would recline on the mats, sweating themselves clean.

The Sakurai seashore, at Imabari in Ehime Prefecture, is the site of a surviving stone bath. A large and spacious hole excavated in a rock wall, the origin of this bath is said to date back to the beginning of the Edo era some four hundred years ago. Though it is not known exactly when the stone baths were first used in Japan, the methodology employed at the Sakurai stone bath provides a glimpse into the lengthy history of the bathing customs of the Japanese people.

Even today the stone bath at the Sakurai seashore is in service from July through September every year, and is crowded with bathers day and night. In addition to the cave that has been open for mixed bathing since its inception, a smaller bath for women was drilled during the Meiji era in order to segregate the sexes. It is dark inside and rather hot immediately after the fuel has burnt. Twenty armfuls of dried fern leaves are burnt at each firing. In the old days, seaweed is said to have been used together with mats soaked in sea water to generate the steam, which the bathers believed to have medicinal efficacies.

Kunio Yanagida[31], a famous folklorist, tried to trace a connection between the origin of the term *furo* (bath) and *muro,* which is synonymous with "cave" or "rock hole," and contended that *muro* had been corrupted to *furo.*

Unquestionably, the stone bath at Sakurai appears to symbolize this etymology. In any event, the indigenous stone bath may well be the original form of the steam bath in Japan. For this reason, its primitive form is now attracting the attention of historians.

There are a number of stories that provide insights into the history of the steam baths. In the Kamakura era, about 800 years ago, a high-ranking priest by the name of *Thyunzyoubou Tyougen*[32] served at *Todaiji* Temple in Nara. He is a well-known figure in the history of Japanese architecture for his contribution to the reconstruction of Todaiji *Garan*[33], a Buddhist cathedral which burned down in 1180. To collect lumber for the reconstruction of the savaged temple he traveled as far

1. The exterior of a stone bath at Sakurai, Imabari City, Ehime Prefecture (Tourism Section, Industries Department, Imabari City).

This was hollowed out of a natural rock formation, with small ventilation apertures in the rear. The exterior of the bath is presently reinforced with concrete.

2. The interior of the same bath.

This bath is 7.9 meters long, 3 meters high and 3.3 meters wide. The ladie's bath is a little smaller. On the side opposite the entrance there is a small opening in the stone which served as a skylight.

3. An existing stone bath in the Saba River basin, Suo-no-kuni; Noya, Tokuchi-cho, Saba-gun.

This is an example of the most primitive type of stone bath. It is about 2.7 meters long and about 1.9 meters wide.

as Yamaguchi, at the western tip of Japan's main island, Honshu. In villages near the forests where, according to legend, he cut wood, the tradition of the stone bath is still to be found. He is said to have constructed a number of bathing places as recreational and dispensary facilities for the workers involved in cutting or transporting the building materials.

Of course, the facilities now available are not original. However, a bath at Noya, Tokuchi, Saba-gun, Yamaguchi Prefecture vividly represents the style of Kamakura era stone baths. It retains the most primitive form of its kind, in that stones are piled up around a recess in a huge rock to create a spacious interior. This stone bath, located to the side of a stream in a ravine far from human habitation, can rightfully be associated with the exploits of the dedicated bonze.

In and around this area the stone bath introduced by the priest has been adopted for use in the homes of local residents, though its form has been changed slightly, and a number of home-made stone baths are to be found. The one at Kishimi, for example, consists of an echinus of stones plastered outside with mud with a small opening in its facade. Though most of these baths located at farm houses are no longer in service, some are actually still being used. These home-made stone baths seem to have been installed later by people who employed the Noya stone bath as a model for their own bathing facilities.

Instead of individual bathrooms at their homes, the people of Tokuchi town now use a large ironwork public stone bath with an attached furnace house. Arriving alone or in groups, residents enjoy steam bathing before refreshing themselves with beer together with fellow bathers seated around the hearth sunken in the *tatami* (rush mat) floor. In this town, the public stone bathhouse is playing an important role as a communication center which promotes recreation and intimacy among the citizenry.

There are also steam baths made of dried mud in place of stones. A well-known example is the *kama-buro* or kiln bath at an inn in *Yase*[34], Sakyo-ku, Kyoto, which has been constructed as a precise model of an Edo era bath, reproducing exactly the baths of several hundred years ago.

The kiln bath, 1.8 meters high, is shaped like a hillock and accommodates two or three bathers. The method of heating employed is basically the same as that used for stone baths, with pine and other evergreen leaves being burnt in the fuel hole. When the leaves have completely burnt, the ashes are removed and mats laid on the stone floor, which has been dampened with salt water. The steam generated by the fresh evergreen leaves and the salt water are believed to have medicinal effects. Records from the middle ages say that court nobles and warriors habitually used the Yase kiln bath for long periods of spa-treatment.

Today at Yase there is a new kiln bath, built for tourists, which is fueled with heavy oil to keep its interior temperature at 50 to 60 degrees centigrade. This temperature, far lower than that of a sauna, is comfortable for bathers even if they spend long periods lying on the mats, and expedites pleasant perspiration. After spending some time in the kiln bath, patrons retire to the hot water of the attached conventional bathtub and wash the sweat from their bodies.

4. Another stone bath, at Kishimi.
Stones were piled into a mound, and the exterior with loam. The interior is about 2.8 meters long, about 2.4 meters wide, and about 1.7 meters high. The wall is roughly 0.5-0.7 meters thick.

5. Contemporary stone bath in the Saba River basin, Suo-no-kuni, with a steel structure.

The stone bath tradition is still alive here. A large stone bath was constructed with a steel structure, and is now popular as a public bath for the village.

6. Interior of the contemporary stone bath in the Saba River basin.

This stone bath is so spacious that about 20 peoples can bath at once.

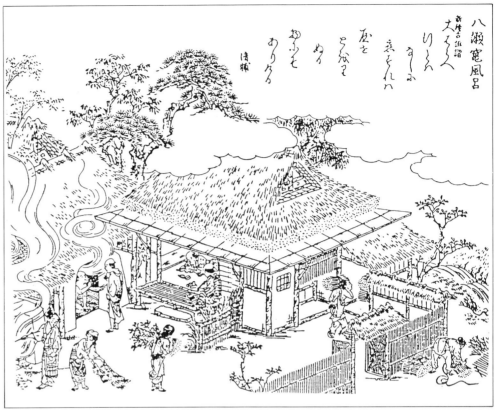

7. *Kama-buro* at Yase (Courtesy of the Society for the Diffusion of fine Books)

Miyako-meisho-zue, a popular book featuring geographical descriptions of Kyoto with drawings and pictures published in 1780, shows that there were seven or eight *kama-buro* in those days. The bath is depicted in two views in which heating the bath and bathing are shown, respectively. They also show that the bathhouse was thatch-roofed.

9. The firebox opening of the kamaburo at Yase.

It is 1.8 meters high, mound-shaped, and its interior floorspace is equivalent to about three *ta-tami* floor mats (one mat is about one meter by two meters). The floor is paved with flat stones.

8. Today's *kamaburo* at Yase. This bath is structurally identical to the ancient *kamaburo* at Yasc, making it an update version of that bath. It remains a popular bath even today.

Buddhism and Bathing

From the foregoing it is clear that the traditional steam bath has survived in Japan, although in limited locations.

Temples and the living quarters of priests, on the other hand, were equipped with baths in order to obey the tenets of Buddhism, which hold that bathing removes seven ills and bestows seven blessings. Bathing was also fully taken advantage of in the promotion of Buddhism among the general populace. The bathrooms of temples were frequently opened to supply the populace with opportunities for bathing, a practice known as *seyoku* or the provision of charity baths. For example, in 1192, during the Kamakura era, *Minamo-tono Yoritomo*[35], then the warlord ruler of the country, offered a grand *seyoku* for 100 days to 10,000 people in total. In 1225, the Kamakura *Bakufu* (government) sponsored a similar event in honor of *Hojo Masako*[36], wife of the ruler.

The grand bathhouse of *Todaiji* Temple, which had been reconstructed by *Thyunzyoubou Tyougen* at the beginning of the Kamakura era and renewed again in 1239, was also opened to the public. Large bathhouses are generally subject to rapid deterioration due to water and fire being used in great quantities. The bathhouse of *Todaiji* Temple, which has survived until today after being repaired a number of times, is the oldest and the largest of its kind in Japan.

At the center of the bathhouse is a large iron tub of two meters in diameter, formerly sunk in the ground (it is now placed on the floor). A small structure called a *furo-yakata* houses the tub and retains the heat inside. The facade of the *furo-yakata* is decorated with a unique and amusing roof member called a *karahafu*. At the rear of the *furo-yakata* is a large space on the floor for a furnace, where a large cauldron is believed to have been placed to heat and supply water to the bathtub.

"Hokkekyo Mandara Ezu" (fig. 13) is a drawing which dates from 1327 (toward the end of the Kamakura era) which vividly illustrates how much people enjoyed *seyoku:* pedestrians, abandoning their baggage on the street, are rushing into the bathhouse. *Seyoku* was an invaluable and irreplaceable means of satisfying the demand for bathing facilities before public baths (known as *sento*) became common. In this picture, we can see a large bathtub to which water is supplied from a cauldron in the rear in the same way as at the grand bathhouse of *Todaiji* Temple. Bathers are wearing cloths wrapped around their waists; nude bathing, a popular custom since the Edo era, was not a habit in those days.

There were two types of temple bathhouses used for *seyoku*. One was the immersion type like those of *Todaiji* and *"Hokkekyo Mandara Ezu"* (fig. 13), and the other was the sudatorium (hot-air sweat bath) type. The bathhouse of *Myoshinji* Temple in Kyoto is a typical example of the latter. This house was originally built for the repose of the soul of *Akechi Mitsuhide*[37], a warrior who was affiliated with this temple, and was remodeled in the Edo era into its present form.

The bathhouse was refined and made extremely functional in the Edo era. At the center was the *furo-yakata* for steam bathing, with a *karahafu* on the front wall and three doors below cleverly contrived to allow bathers to pass through and adjust the quantity of the steam in the room. Under the *sunoko-bari* (raised slat) floor of the *furo-yakata,* a cauldron was placed on the furnace. When the steam from the cauldron had sufficiently filled the house, the sudatorium opened. In the back of the house was a fuel hole for the main furnace. A second furnace was installed to its side, to heat *kakari-yu*[38], or the fresh hot water with which bathers cleansed themselves at the conclusion of the bath.

On every anniversary of *Akechi Mitsuhide's* death the bathhouse was open to the public, as *seyoku,* long into the Edo era. The bath was known as *Akechi-buro* though the date at which it took this name is unknown.

10. The exterior of bathhouse in *Todaiji* Temple.

The building faces west with its entrance on the gabled side. It is done in the *irimoya-zukuri* style (a hipped and gabled roof) on three sides and *kirizuma-zukuri* style (a pitched and gabled roof) in the back. In the front there is an opening which measures one *ken* (about two meters). This is the largest of existing remaines.

11. The bathhouse in *Todaiji* Temple.

A *furo-yakata* done in the *karahafu* style (a Chinese-style gable) is located to the east of the room's center. The *karahafu* style for the front of the *furoyakata* was later utilized for public baths as well as for steam-bath houses in *Zen* temples.

12. The interior of the *Todaiji* Temple *furo-yakata*.

The *furo-yakata* was built for the purpose of conserving the warmth of the bath. In the center was buried an iron bathtub bearing an inscription of the year 1197.

13. *"Hokkekyo Mandara Ezu"* (pictures and drawings on the *hokke-mandara* sutra) owned by *Honpoji* Temple, Toyama Prefecture. (Photo: by courtesy of KAO corporation)

This was painted in 1327, near the end of the Kamakura period. A depiction of *seyoku* from *"Hokkekyo Mandara Ezu."*

"Hokkekyo Mandara Ezu": the 22nd work, 13th scroll. The bath is thought to have been prepared by taking hot water from a large furnace located in the rear and carrying the water to the ladle over the bathtub through a pipe.

14. The exterior of the *Akechi-buro* at *Myoshinji* Temple.

The structure is of the *kirizuma-zukuri* style (a pitched and gables roof), presenting a beautiful exterior appearance which features a *karahafu* in the center.

15. The interior of the bathhouse at *Myoshinji* Temple.

16. The boiler at *Myoshinji* Temple.

The mechanism for sending steam into the bath house includes two boilers, which seem to have been used for preparing *kakari-yu* (fresh hot water to pour over the body).

17. The bathhouse in *Myoshinji* Temple.

Inside the building, a *karahafu*-style bathhouse is located in the center. Its front wall features useful three-layer sliding doors which combine both entrance and steam control functions.

The History of Sento

Sento, or public baths, have an unrivaled place in the history of the Japanese bath. *Seyoku* at the temples was also a sort of public bath. In Kyoto, public baths for which people paid money were already in existence toward the end of the Kamakura era.

According to the Muromachi era diaries of *kuge* (members of the aristocracy), even the nobility patronized public baths. However, they seem to have hired public baths together with relatives and colleagues of their own class exclusively, to avoid bathing with the lower social classes.

We can see a *sento* in *"Rakuchu-rakugai-zu Byobu"* (pictures of scenes in and around the capital drawn on folding screens), which beautifully represent the bustling streets of Kyoto in those days. On the road along a river in one picture, pedestrians are walking up and down amid children at play. Behind the gate, there is a shingle-roofed *sento,* presumably a sudatoria, which is not so large but seems to be crowded with bathers. To its rear is depicted a well bucket used to draw water.

The next picture shows many more details of the interior of a public bath. In the washing area depicted in the foreground, a *yuna* (female bathhouse attendant) is washing a man's back. This was an indispensable service at public baths in those days. The rear of the washing area is partitioned by a plate wall. A man is coming out the door at the corner of the wall.

Inside the bathhouse is a steam bath equipped with a sliding door to confine the steam within the room, in the typical style of this period known as *todana-buro,* or closet bath, supposedly in association with the built-in furniture of its configuration.

It is said that *sento* got their start in Edo (present-day Tokyo), the capital during the Edo era, in 1591 when *Iseno Yoichi* built a bathhouse at the foot of a bridge and collected money from bathers. The business was a success, since curiosity-seekers were drawn in numbers. A record from that period notes that there were quite a few cus-tomers who were not accustomed to the new fashion and complained that "drips are so hot that my nose is blocked and I can't speak." This suggests that the public baths at the beginning of the Edo era were steam baths.

The number of public baths increased in Edo, because people declined to have baths at their homes in order to reduce fire hazards and also out of economic considerations. With houses made of wood and packed cheek by jowl, Edo repeatedly suffered disastrous fires. Once a fire broke out it quickly became an inferno in the wooden city, so people avoided fire hazards as much as possible. Public baths were also necessary and economical for merchants who had a number of resident employees.

Above all, *sento* provided pleasures and enjoyment that people could never experience at home baths. From early in the morning people visited the public baths, which were in service from 6 a.m. to 6 p.m., sometimes competing with their friends to be the first arrival. Neighborhood men and women, young and old alike, gathered to bathe naked in the absence of class discrimination and exchange the latest gossip and rumors in the companionship of nudity. Though quarrels or crimes may occasionally have occurred, *sento* were irreplaceable recreation centers for the ordinary people who had few entertainment options, unlike the satiated Japanese of today.

In the Edo era, men and women bathed together at most of the public baths, which posed various problems. The government frequently issued ordinances to ban the embarrassing practice, but these were hardly abided by in the early days. In the latter half of the era, however, public baths appeared which separated the sexes by space or by time sharing, while others accommodated women only, as the result of the repeated enactment of regulations. In Kyoto and Osaka, however, washing areas and dressing rooms continued to be used in common by both men and women for some time, though the bathtubs had been segregated.

18. *"Rakuchu-rakugai-zu Byobu"* (pictures of Kyoto and its environs on a folding screen) owned by Yonezawa city Educational Committee of Yamagata Prefecture.

19. A scene from the second floor parlor of a bathhouse, early in the Meiji era (*"Fuzoku Gaho"* published in March 1905) (Owned by National Diet Library)

Beginning around the middle of Edo era, public bathhouses commonly featured tatami-floored parlors for male customers on the second floor. They served as recreational clubs for men, and were crowded with bathers enjoying the post-bath afterglow at length. However, since around 1885(Meiji 18) they have gradually disappeared as bathhouse style underwent change. (From *"Meiji Jibutsu Kigen"* by *Ishii Kendou*)

20. "Nagoyajo Taimenjo Jodan-no-ma-no Goten Shoji Koshibarie" (pictures on the decorative paper skirting of a paper sliding door in the upper chamber of the meeting place at Nagoya Castle)—A *todana-buro* styled public bath (owned by Nagoya Castle). The painter's name is unknown, although it is said to be the work of *Kano Tanyu*[39]. It depicts *yuna* (literally "women of the bath") who washed customer's backs.

Foreigners who came to Japan in the Edo era were taken aback by the incredible frankness regarding the body, let alone the passion for cleanliness and the predilection to bathing of the Japanese people.

The pleasures of a *sento* were multiplied by the pastimes available at the *tatami* parlor on the second floor. After bathing, men would drink tea, eat cakes, and play *go* (a Japanese board game) and *shogi* (Japanese chess) with their acquaintants in a state of semi-nudity. At every *sento* there were at least a few retired notables from the neighborhood who would leisurely oscillate between the bath and the second floor the whole day long. Thus, the second floor served as a refuge for leisure or a social club for the district, adding another key role for the *sento* in the community. The bona fide practice of semi-naked companionship continued into the early days in the Meiji era.

What typifies the *sento* style of the Edo era is not limited to the above. The sudatorium, or *todanaburo* in most cases, is not very convenient as a public bath if a large number of people frequently moves back and forth through the entrance door. Another system was invented, therefore, to confine the bathtub to a chamber with a low communicating door called *zakuro-guchi* ("pomegranate door"), which bathers were required to stoop through when passing to and from the outer washing area. This device was designed to limit the flow of air through the room. The facade of the chamber was decorated in different ways at different bathhouses, which competed with each other to present the most attractive ornamentation. There were two types of *zakuro-guchi*, the *karahafu* style of *Todaiji* temple's *furo-yakata* and the *torii* (Shinto shrine archway) style.

The bathtub in the chamber was filled with hot water to a shallow depth, in which a bather immersed the lower half of the body while simultaneously exposing the upper half to the densely steamy atmosphere. The door was kept closed to retain the steam, allowing little light to enter.

Nothing was visible through the thick steam. It was difficult even to see whether the water in the bathtub was clean enough. Men and women bathed together. It could not be denied that this disorderliness posed some problems from hygienic and moral perspectives.

There were fanciful *sento* styles, too. A public bath was not necessarily required to have a permanent structure. The simplest were bathtubs placed on the roadside. Pictures of such makeshift public baths leave little doubt that people in those days were quite open-minded regarding public nudity.

Another version of the *sento* was a boat with an on-board bathtub which would moor alongside a sightseeing ship crowded with passengers. This floating public bath seemed to have attained great success, since sightseers did not need to land for bathing. Nothing but such witty ideas, which appeared one after another, can convey in detail the enthusiasm of the populace for bathing.

In the middle of the Meiji era, *zakuro-guchi* were banned and subsequently the sudatoria gradually gave way to immersion baths. "Improved bathrooms" appeared around this time and public bathhouses became cleaner and more hygienic. The development of water supply systems also facilitated the changeover to such a water-consuming bathing practice.

The most distinctive feature of the public bath in modern times has been the design of bathhouse exteriors. The entrance is decorated with *karahafu*, which was used for *Todaiji* temple's *furo-yakata* and the *zakuro-guchi* of Edo-era public baths. The entrance surmounted by *karahafu* has been passed down from the grand bathhouse of *Todaiji* to become the symbol of the public bath. The exterior of the bathhouse is attractively configured in the *shoin-zukuri* style of the palace and the warrior residences of the Edo era. This appearance remained typical throughout the Taisho and Showa eras, but it is a pity that such public bathhouses are now gradually disappearing one after another.

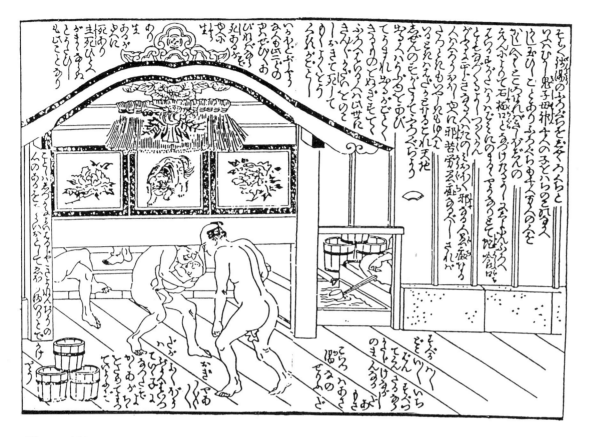
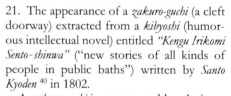

21. The appearance of a *zakuro-guchi* (a cleft doorway) extracted from a *kibyoshi* (humorous intellectual novel) entitled *"Kengu Irikomi Sento-shinwa"* ("new stories of all kinds of people in public baths") written by *Santo Kyoden* [40] in 1802.

A *zakuro-guchi* is constructed by placing a board from the ceiling down to near the floor, and people had to stoop to pass through the low doorway thus created. The idea arose from an attempt to conserve the heat of the bath. The front of each *zakuro-guchi* had a decoration which the public bathhouse was proud of.

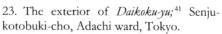

22. An improved bath of the Meiji era from *"Tokyo fuzoku-shi,"* a history of manners and customs in Tokyo published in 1901.

The bath is divided into two parts (men's and women's) by wooden walls, and both the drain floor and the rectangular bathtub are made of wood. It was not until the 1920's that tiled baths came into common use as first the floors of washing areas and the separating walls, and later the bathtubs, were tiled. The hot water for the bath is said to have been *kusuri-yu* (hot water with a bath liquid added), which was afterwards replaced by *shira-yu* (hot water without any additives).

23. The exterior of *Daikoku-yu;* [41] Senju-kotobuki-cho, Adachi ward, Tokyo.

Built entirely of Japanese cypress, this *sento* dates from 1929 and has a gorgeous external appearance. It is an example of the style typical of public baths.

The Pleasures of Bathing

The pleasure of bathing is not limited to enjoying a thorough sweat in a steam bath or sauna, nor to soaking oneself at leisure in a bathtub. The greatest pleasure is in the refreshed feeling one experiences after bathing. In typical urban residences, which have been compared by critics to rabbit hutches, bathrooms inevitably are the smallest rooms and public-bath style lounges are out of the question. After bathing, only the simple pleasures of drinking cold beer and appreciating the subdued pleasantness which follows a bath are available. However, it is beyond doubt that bathing really enhances the enjoyment of drinking a glass of beer. Salaried workers often make "bath to beer" a rule of the day. This demonstrates how highly the Japanese people evaluate the brief spell after taking a bath to soak away the fatigue and stress that follow a day's work. A shower can never substitute for the bath in this respect.

As referred to above, the parlor on the second story of the public bathhouse was the entertainment center of the community in the Edo era. There were some people of certain classes who had private facilities of the same nature, and the remains of such properties may yet be found in Kyoto. In a corner of the precincts of *Nishi-Honganji* Temple, a gorgeous three-story residence known as *Hiunkaku* (literally, " flying cloud structure") stands near a calm pond. Built at the beginning of the Edo era, the home displays an exquisite asymmetric profile and is one of the historic structures that profoundly bespeak of the Japanese aesthetic sensibility.

Hiunkaku has an attached bathhouse called *Oukakudai* (literally "yellow crane stand"), consisting of two wings which contain the bathroom and a parlor facing the pond. This is the oldest steam bathhouse remaining in Japan.

The wooden floor of the bathroom has a drainage channel at its center. At the innermost part of the bathroom, there is a *furo-yakata* for steam bathing and a water tank and a cauldron for heating the *kakari-yu*. The *furo-yakata,* with its *karahafu* room and fine ornamentation, is one of the most beautiful surviving examples of its kind in the country. It is basically the same structure as that of the bathroom of *Myoshinji* Temple, but a little smaller, accommodating three to four persons.

The adjacent parlor is a mezzanine bounded on three sides by verandas and facing the pond, producing an open and spacious ambiance. It is simple enough and does not exert its formality, providing a space in which bathers could rest and cool themselves as they wished after the bath. For the Japanese of those days, there would not have been any pastime surpassing the luxury of enjoying the afterglow of a bath in the *Oukakudai* parlor, fused into the scenery of the surrounding Japanese garden.

The scale of *Oukakudai* is sufficient to serve as the personal bathhouse of *Hiunkaku's* owner though too extravagant by present-day Japanese standards. In *Oukakudai,* however, we can grasp a hint of the unfathomable passion of those born with a profound love of bathing.

24. The exterior of *Hiunkaku*.

Also known as *Hiuntei,* it is a vital part of *Honganji* Temple used for meetings, ceremonies, leisure activities and entertaining high-ranking visitors. It is said to have been moved from *Jurakudai* to be reconstructed.

25. The exterior of *Oukakudai*.

This is done in *yosemune-zukuri* style (a hipped roof) and is shingled. Behind it is a tiled bath in the *kirizuma* style (a gabled roof). The two are connected with a double sliding door.

26. The interior of *Oukakudai*.

Inside the building is a *karahafu* steam-bath house. To the right are a boiler and a tub to provide fresh hot water for use after steam bathing.

27. Interior of veranda at *Oukakudai*. After bathing, guests can spend a relaxing time enjoying the beautiful views from *Oukakudai* and cool themselves off.

Houseguests and the Bath

Such exquisite bathing facilities were created not only for the purpose of pursuing pleasure by the owner himself. They were also indispensable for the entertainment of guests, part of an established social protocol, as is seen in some provinces even at present though on a limited scale.

To recommend bathing upon his guest's arrival was the greatest hospitality the host could render. Hence, most of the residences of warriors and village headmen had bathrooms on the grounds which were not used by family members but were reserved for the exclusive use of guests.

In the Ikoma district of Nara there is a large farmhouse built in the latter half of the 17th century (which has been designated an important cultural property), now owned by Mr. *Naka,* a descendant of a prestigious warrior family of the district. At the rear of the parlor which was used to receive warrior officers is a lavatory and a *furo* for visitors. Though capable of serving only one person, the bath is a full-fledged *todana-buro* type steam bath with a cauldron under the *sunoko-bari* floor like those of *Myoshinji* and *Oukakudai.* This compact *furo* is one of the few remaining steam baths used to entertain guests at farmhouses during the Edo era.

In addition to the steam bath, there were also various other sorts of guest baths to be found during this period. The simplest version was a small room attached to the parlor, with a wooden floor and a drainage channel at its center, to which a bucket of *kakari-yu* was brought for the guest to cleanse himself. A typical example of such simple guest baths is the *furo* owned by the Sasaki family, which has a long lineage in Nagano prefecture. In olden times bathrooms with wooden *sunoko-bari* floors for *kakari-yu* were more prevalent than steam baths, which required a more complicated mechanism including *furo-yakata*. However, the steam bath claimed a practical advantage in that bathing could be enjoyed with small quantities of water.

28. *Todana-buro* at the Naka's residence.
This is a compact steam-bath house in the *to-dana-buro* style, 1.4 meters high and about 1 meter wide and deep. Under the bath house is a furnace with a copper boiler used to generate steam. In front of the bathhouse entrance is a slatted floor upon which bathers can rinse themselves.

29. The bath of the former Sasaki residence, Nagano Prefecture.
The main house was built in 1731, while the premises and the bath were added in 1747. The bathroom has a wooden floor with a channel in the center. Hot water was brought in by pail for rinsing after bathing.

Home Baths

Most farmers in prewar times made their own steam baths at their homes. Since their labors from early morning till late in the evening prohibited them from drawing quantities of water from the well or heating it for long periods, a number of one-person steam baths employing buckets were invented in various districts.

There are amusing steam baths known as *fugo-buro*, at farmhouses in the Iga district of Mie prefecture in central Japan, which consist of a bucket placed on the furnace on the earthen floor with a cover made of a straw basket called a *fugo* hung from above.

In the provinces from the Kohoku district north of Lake Biwa in Shiga prefecture to the Hokuriku area on the Sea of Japan, there are steam baths shaped like barrels which are called *mugi-buro* (literally "wheat bath"). These feature an entrance door to the side. A furnace is placed under the floor to fill the room with steam. Such simple, closed-type *furo* are well-suited to colder climates as they require little in the way of water and fuel.

In these steam chambers, bathers warmed themselves long enough to loosen the filth from the body before scraping it off and allowing it to sink into the bathtub to dirty the water. The waste water thus produced was not discarded but rather was recycled as fertilizer. A larger quantity of filth makes for better fertilizer, so it was not desirable to change the water in the tub too frequently if hygiene could be ignored. Thus, farmhouse baths served not only for bathing farmers but also functioned as small-scale sources of fertilizer together with lavatories, serving the national interest by raising agricultural production.

These steam baths have now almost entirely disappeared. Given today's highly developed water supply system, their advantage of bathing efficiently with small quantities of water is no longer meaningful. Another factor which expedited their extinction may be the complex mechanisms required to produce and contain the steam.

The original of the present *furo* is what is called the *sue-buro* (literally, a fixed bath), a barrel filled with hot water. Exactly when did it debut on its way to replacing the steam bath?

A *karasu*(crow)-*tengu* (long-nosed goblin) from the Kamogawa River in Kyoto is bathing in the last scene of the *"Zegaibo-eshi"* drawn in the 14th century. The injured *tengu* is immersed in a bath tub made of hollowed wood. This picture is very important in tracing the origin of the present-day system in which bathtubs are directly heated. In this picture, hot water is still being supplied to the bathtub by a pipe from the cauldron on the furnace placed in the rear. The advent of the direct heating system which incorporates a furnace in the bathtub seems to have taken place in the Edo era at the earliest. Before that, even the *sue-buro* had required such a cumbersome mechanism.

Two typical *sue-buro* baths are *Goemon-buro* (Goemon's bath) and *teppo-buro* (literally "gun bath"). A *Goemon-buro* is an iron bathtub placed directly on a furnace. The outer surfaces of the bathtub and the furnace are plastered in order to retain heat efficiently. Since the Meiji era the *Goemon-buro* has been further refined and now prevails over Japan assuming the position of the representative Japanese *furo*.

The *Goemon-buro* has been very popular among the Japanese people. It was taken up in the *"Tokaidochu Hizakurige,"* a widely known sketch of travels along the Tokaido route written by *Jippensha Ikku* in the Edo era. *Yaji-san* and *Kita-san,* who were born and raised in Edo, stayed at an inn in Odawara town. Since *Goemon-buro* were not common in Edo at that time (which is proved by historical records available today), they did not know how to use the bath. A wooden plate floats in the *Goemon-buro* bathtub, and a bather is supposed to submerge it to the bottom with his or her body weight and remain on it as protection from the heated bottom. However, the pair mistook the plate for a cover and removed it. The bottom was

30. A *fugo-buro* at Saga.

After the furnace had been built an iron boiler was installed on which a bathtub was set. The woven-straw lid called a *fugo* is raised and lowered by rope and pulley. The bottom of the tub is covered with a kind of slat floor called a *sana (sunoko)* on which the bather squats. The *fugo* is then lowered to serve as a cover. This kind of bath is also called a *tobikomi-buro* (literally "plunging diving bath"), as one seems to plunge into the bath.

31. A *mugi-buro* at Ohmi

The deep, barrel-shaped bathtub has a hinged lid and an opening to one side. It is heated by a furnace located underneath. With its tight-fitting cover, this sort of bath helps conserve both water and fuel and furthermore requires only simple support facilities. Thus, this kind of bath is well-suited to cool climates.

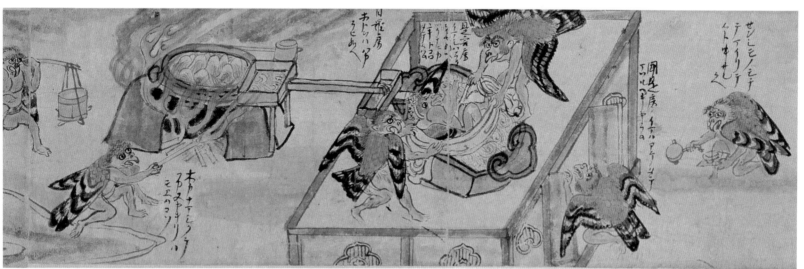

32. A bath tub where hot water is carried through a pipe; from *"Zegaibo-eshi"* (picture scrolls with explanatory notes and stories on *Zegaibo*) by *Kamo Kahan* (owned by *Manjuin*, photo by Kyoto National Museum)
This shows in detail how to take hot water by a ladle from a boiler through a pipe to the bathtub.

too hot to touch with their feet and, at the end of their wits, they entered the bathtub wearing *geta* (wooden clogs), eventually breaking the bottom of the tub. This is only one of the fiascoes the merry twosome created during the course of their travels.

The *teppo-buro* has rivaled the *Goemon-buro* as a home bath since the Edo era. A gun-like copper furnace is positioned vertically at the corner of the barrel-shaped tub. Charcoal is supplied from above and air is drawn from below into the furnace to generate heat. When the water is heated sufficiently, a tile is placed on the top of the furnace to adjust the fire. The furnace is so hot that it is partitioned by a plate to protect the bather's body.

Teppo-buro were very popular due to their portability, as they could be moved anywhere unlike *Goemon-buro*. Even in the Edo era, when public bathhouses were found everywhere, *teppo-buro* baths were said to have been leased to those who could not find time to patronize a *sento*.

Other types of baths included the *Tsujiburo,* for which water was heated and used in a bathtub placed on a busy street *"Edo Nyuyoku Hyaku-sugata"* (fig. 35), and the *Ninaiburo,* a bathtub which was transported to places where people congregated and served as a public bath set under a tree. Such portable public baths were installed on boats as well, and all variations were regarded as new businesses which brought in fares.

Nowadays, *Goemon-buro* and *teppo-buro* are hardly to be found. However, these two types of baths are the ancestors most akin to the modern home bath, and played a vital role in disseminating the practice of installing baths in individual residences.

Steam baths are now almost extinct, except in a few districts as referred to above. Contemporary Japanese might be surprised to know of the glorious record the steam bath maintained until a few centuries ago. For this reason, the more thoroughly should we remember what the steam bath for the people in the long history of the Japanese bath.

33. The bath on board a ship of Edo; from *"Wakansenyo-shu,"* an anthology of remarks on Chinese and Japanese ships written by *Kanazawa Kenko* in 1870. These simple facilities featured a *sue-buro* (fixed bath) on a boat. According to an essay entitled *"Kotto-shu"* by *Santo Kyoden,* however, passengers had to pay not only for bathing but for meals and accommodation as well. In addition, a tax was imposed.

34. Staying at Odawara, from *"Dochu Hizakurige"* by *Ando Hiroshige* (from "Edo-jidai Zushi" Vol. 14).

An Ukiyoe print. by *Ando Hiroshige*, sketching an episode featuring *Yaji-san* and *Kita-san* with a *Goemon-buro*. (Owned by Kanagawa Prefectural Museum)

35. *Tsuji-buro* and *ninai-buro*; from *"Edo Nyuyoku Hyaku Sugata,"* ("a hundred aspects of bathing in Edo") by Kazuo Hanasaki

The *tsuji-buro* was designed to give passersby an opprtunity to bathe by placing a bathtub in a busy street and heating it there. On the other hand, the *ninai-buro* was a mobile compact public bath and could be carried to a bustling locale and installed in the shade of a tree so that people could enjoy a bath right there.

36. *Teppo-buro* at Yanai City, Yamaguchi Prefecture.

A copper heater surrounded by a hoop and shaped like a *teppo* (gun) passes vertically through one end of the wooden bathtub. Charcoal is added from above, and air admitted from the *otoshi* (false bottom) below to make a fire. After the bath has been sufficiently heated the intensity of the fire can be regulated by placing a tile across the opening of the heater. It is very dangerous to touch the gun-shaped part, which becomes extremely warm.

Chapter III

THE EFFICACY
OF
BATHING

Bath Life for a Comfortable Life

All human beings, regardless of race or life style, are nurtured for nine months in the lukewarm bath of the mother's amniotic fluid in the womb, an environment which could be called "the bath of life." For the unborn child it is a most comfortable springboard to existance, providing safety while allowing free and natural movement. This is the very first physical experience we all encounter: a wonderful "bath life".

While bathing, we can recover our normal physical rhythm because we can relax and regain our mental composure. It cannot be denied that the attraction and efficacy of bathing lie herein.

It is well known throughout the world that Japanese people love bathing and are sticklers for cleanliness. Foreign writers who visited Japan, both hundreds of years ago and more recently, were amazed by this. They proclaimed the Japanese to be the people who are more enthusiastic about maintaining their personal hygiene than any other in the world. However, the Japanese practice of bathing is not difficult to understand. Living in a land blessed by numerous hot springs, the Japanese people are very familiar with bathing in these spas and thus enjoy a life style which incorporates warm water baths. This practice could be termed their wisdom of the art of living.

Some people claim that this aspect of the Japanese lifestyle is related to the way the weather and climate of the Japanese archipelago contributed to the formation of the nation's culture. However, it is the writer's personal belief that the real source of such a lifestyle lies in the first bath which all people without exception experience before birth. It is reasonable to conclude that the impulse to this practice is a psychological phenomenon or natural desire which is possessed by all human beings.

Basil Hall Chamberlain, who visited Japan in 1873, comments in his book entitled "Things Japanese" that the Japanese practice of taking a daily bath to maintain personal cleanliness was an exceptionally attractive practice of all people living in Japan. In fact, some visitors from Europe or the United States have been captivated by bathing in hot springs or public baths in Japan, and have chosen Japanese-style bathrooms for their homes in admiration of the Japanese lifestyle.

Almost all Japanese have a bath when they get back home after a hard day's work,. It is a typical feature of the Japanese life-style to wash away completely the day's fatigue by taking a bath, and never to leave it until the next day. Bathing plays a more important role than ever in the contemporary age, enabling people to relax and recover the healthy life rhythms which otherwise are likely to be lost in a complex and difficult society with its harsh business environment, which causes both mental and physical fatigue.

This chapter will address the effects of bathing and some of the scientific reasons for them, and introduce useful knowledge and examples of correct bathing methods. It is hoped that this will contribute to helping the world's people to share an appreciation for a pleasant and healthy bath life.

The Science of Bathing and Health

There is no need to dwell on the fact that bathing has the effect of washing off sweat and dirt, keeping us clean as well as warm. However, we can expect different changes and benefits for various parts of our bodies depending on the bathing method, water temperature, length of bathing time, water quality and the depth of the bath tub.

What are the physiological and psychological effects of bathing? Recent studies and tests regarding these matters have clarified the relationship between bathing and health mechanisms in a scientific manner.

If we can make proper use of the results of such researches and the knowledge of traditional hot spring cures, we can expect wonderful benefits from bathing in terms of maintaining and advancing mental and physical health and beauty, curing disease, and rehabilitation. Even though the Japanese love bathing, only few are in possession of correct knowledge about bathing and the maintenance of good health.

Physical Characteristics and Effects of Bathing

The basic characteristics of bathing can be broadly divided into three categories:

Thermal characteristics
Hydrostatic pressure characteristics
Buoyancy characteristics

Thermal Characteristics of Bathing

We can warm ourselves by bathing. This is the basic thermal characteristic. Heat from warm water penetrates through the skin to the viscera and the brain—through the muscles, the blood vessels, the digestive system and the circulatory system—affecting the nervous system to produce physiological and psychological effects.

Warm Water Bathing and Physiological and Psychological Changes

In general, humans are insensible to water whose temperature is close to body temperature (between 35° and 37°C), and these water temperatures produce the least stimulation to our bodies.

If the water temperature is about one degree higher or more, over 38°C, perspiration begins to seep from the hair roots and sweat glands of the skin, from which sweat, oil and dirt are discharged.

Perspiration evaporates from the surface of the skin, cooling it and making us feel refreshed. At the same time, the process of perspiration consumes calories. This is the reason people say "I feel refreshed after taking a bath," "We feel tired after having a long bath," or "Bathing makes me slimmer." In the fully temperature-controlled living environment of today, we sometimes suffer from a lack of natural body temperature regulation, in particular due to the use of air-conditioning. Bathing daily can normalize our skin's ability to regulate body temperature.

Generally, the Japanese prefer a higher water temperature for bathing (42° to 43°C), while it is said that Europeans prefer lower-water temperatures (38° to 41°C).

The Efficacies of Higher Temperature Baths (42° to 44°C)

High water temperatures raise body temperature as the heat penetrates into the body, which helps activate the perspiration process and accelerates natural metabolic activity. In addition, the circulation of the blood through the skin and the muscles is accelerated and the discharge of lactic acid and other fatigue residues generated by sports and other activities is promoted, relieving muscle stiffness and fatigue.

High-temperature bathing accelerates the secretion of adrenalin by stimulating the sympathetic nervous system, intensifies strain, vitalizes the whole body and, all together, these changes affect us very positively in our everyday activities.

The pulse rate and blood flow accelerate immediately when we enter a hot bath. At the same time, blood pressure jumps up because the blood vessels of the heart shrink temporarily. However, blood pressure declines gradually while we are in the bath, because capillary vessels in the skin's surface expand and the blood flow through them increases. Therefore, in some cases blood pressure is lower than normal right after bathing.

Bathing immediately before and after meals should be avoided. The quantity of blood f low on the body surface increases when we have a bath, and blood from the stomach, liver and other internal organs is drawn to the body' s surface.

This results in reduced performance of the internal organs and hampers the digestive and absorptive actions of the stomach and intestines.

The Efficacies of Lukewarm Baths (38° to 40°C)

Bathing in lukewarm water stimulates the parasympathetic nervous system and accelerates the secretion of noradrenaline, which reduces excessive strain and stimulation both psychologically and physiologically. This is the reason we normally feel relaxed and calmed by bathing. Having a bath, we can terminate the day's business and our fatigue will not carry over to the morrow. This is an aspect of the typical Japanese lifestyle.

The effects of lukewarm water bathing appear gradually after entering the bath. When we take a lukewarm bath for a sufficient time, it does not impose any undue load on the circulatory system or the heart. Even people with high blood pressure can reasonably expect their blood pressure to stabilize in the normal range. It is understandable thus that many spa resorts which are famous for their efficacy in combating paralysis employ lukewarm water.

Hydrostatic Pressure

When the body is in a bath tub, it is subject to the pressure of water, or hydrostatic pressure. Therefore, it is said that in the bath the waist and bust shrink by about 3 to 5 cm, and 1 to 2 cm, respectively.

If we spend all day on our feet, the lower part of the body stores water, and the legs swell in par-

ticular, which is a cause of fatigue. In a bath tub, the deeper the water, the larger the hydrostatic pressure is; it pushes up the water stored in the lower part of the legs and alleviates the resultant fatigue. In addition, pressure on the blood and lymphatic vessels help push back their contents to the heart, stimulating and reinforcing heart and lung performance. Also, hydrostatic pressure stimulates and vitalizes the skin and prevents the development of excessive body weight. Hydrostatic pressure produces enhanced effects in Japanese bathtubs, in particular, because they are deeper than European and American tubs.

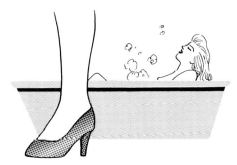

Buoyancy

The body floats in water, due to its buoyancy properties. According to the Archimedean principle, it is said that the weight below the neck when submerged in water is reduced by roughly 85% due to buoyancy. We feel lighter, and can move more easily in water than in air. Therefore, hot-spring rehabilitation is effective for problems such as fractures, lumbago, and cerebral apoplexy. Even people who cannot ordinarily exercise due to overweight or who cannot move smoothly can participate in exercises when they are in the water.

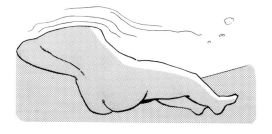

Bathing for Fresh-Looking Skin

It is often said that Japanese women have smooth, beautiful skin. As examples in this volume demonstrate, fresh and comely beauties wearing happy expressions have been portrayed in famous Japanese paintings, *ukiyoe* prints and other depictions of feminine beauty, just after having bathed.

This can be explained by the fact that bathing brings beauty as a reflection of physical health, because blood circulation is stimulated, metabolism is enhanced, and hormone secretion accelerated thanks to the warming produced by bathing.

Bathing and Beautiful Skin

If we make it a habit to repeat, twice a day in the morning and in the evening, a gentle massage with soft towel or sponge from the hands and feet toward the heart during a lukewarm bath (38° to 40°C), we can expect beautiful and fine skin. Also, it ensures a healthy constitution free of the common cold.

As we can see in the pictures of beautiful women after having a bath, skin and hair care is very important after a bath when the skin is alkaline and its pores are open. This is the best time for effective skin treatment, and the lotions and oils which are best for the skin will bring good effects in maintaining a beautiful skin. In fact, the image of a woman concentrating on combing her hair and making up her face is indeed a fascinating one.

Lukewarm water is gentle to the skin. We can enjoy comfortable bathing at warmer temperatures (42° to 44°C) with a good sense according to the season if the water is steeped in sweet flag (Japanese Iris) on Boys' Day, citron hot bath on the winter solstice, or herbs and other bathing additives. In addition to their effect of promoting clear skin, these are part of the traditional Japanese bath life with its wisdom for each season of the year.

The Slimming Efficacy of Bathing

About 60% of the human body consists of water. It is said that overweight people have higher proportions of body fat than other people.

As mentioned in the previous paragraph, when the body becomes one degree warmer while bathing the perspiration process begins. We can loose weight efficiently by the exchange of heat which is caused by perspiration. It accelerates the dissolution of fat within the body, and better results in weight loss efforts. Weight reduction should be less than 3 to 4 kg per month, a reasonable schedule for maintaining good overall health. If we try to loose too much weight at once, we may get wrinkles or experience health problems.

One should take a high temperature bath (42° to 44°C), and when perspiration starts get out bath tub and take a two or three minute break to cool down. Then enter the bath tub again for 4 to 5 minutes. This series of steps should be repeated three times during one bath time.

It is important to have three meals a day regularly, to control calorie intake by following a well-planned menu, and to exercise properly. If these are done in combination, it will greatly accelerate weight loss. (Those who do not feel perfectly healthy need a medical check-up and should consult a physician.)

Bathing twice a day, morning and evening, as one habitual pattern of one's lifestyle will result in weight reduction. We can be slimmer naturally and beautifully when we make this practice a pleasant rhythm of daily life.

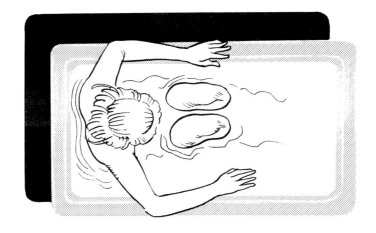

Bathing to Recover a Healthy Rhythm of Life

When suffering discomfort due to irritation or stress or before going to bed, a lukewarm bath (38° to 42°C) for 20 to 30 minutes will make you feel relaxed and calm your temper. A natural rhythm of life will be recovered.

When feeling weary and fatigued, or suffering from a lack of sleep or insufficient exercise, take a high temperature bath (42° to 44°C) for three to four minutes and rest for awhile. Repeat this a few times, and you will feel refreshed and revitalized.

People who have slightly high blood pressure are recommended to take a lukewarm bath for 20 to 30 minutes every day, to lower blood pressure to normal levels without special treatment. Be careful not to take high temperature baths (42° to 44°C), because this makes the blood vessels dilated abruptly. Those suffering from hypertention should seek the advice of a physician.

On the contrary, those suffering from hypotention are recommended to take a short high temperature bath (42° to 44°C) and get out quickly. This style of bathing, done at the same time every day, is good for the blood pressure.

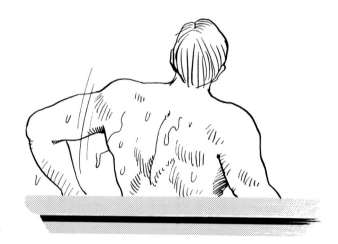

Bathing Additives to Make a Home Bath Like a Spa

The Diffusion of Bathing Additives in Japan

To bring the efficacy of hot spring baths into the home, mineral residues from hot spring pools and similar items were refined and used as bathing additives.

Medicinal plants and fruits were used as household remedies from ancient days. The efficacy of drinking infusions of Chinese traditional medicines was well-known among the Japanese. The benefits of these items have been enhanced by the change from drinking infusions to bathing in warm medicated water.

The analysis of the components of hot spring waters and research into their scents and aromas has made it possible to refine stable and safe preparations which have the same efficacy.

The Efficacy of Bathing Additives

One of the main ingredients of "BATHCRIN" is sodium sulfate (salt cake). It accelerates the blood circulation and metabolism, stimulates the skin and raises its surface temperature, raises body temperature and keeps it warmer.

Another main ingredient is sodium bicarbonate (baking soda), which emulsifies the skin's fats and secretions. It makes the skin smoother and cleaner. There are many spas known as "'beauty spas' making beauty" whose main ingredient is sodium bicarbonate.

One other ingredient, lanolin, retains moisture within the skin and protects its surface. This is what makes the skin feel smooth and moist after taking a bath with "BATHCRIN".

The fragrance and color of "BATHCRIN" impart mental and physical composure.

When bathing additives or herbs are added to freshly heated water, it eases the irritation to the skin which is characteristic of such water. This is good and safe for older and weaker people.

"Medicated Baths" with Extracts of Unrefined Medicines

"BATHCRIN Bathherb" is a medicated bathing additive, with extracts of unrefined natural medicines as its major ingredient. The fragrance unique to these medicines and the color of natural grass imparts us with a feeling of relaxation. It warms the body as well.

The main ingredients of "BATHCRIN Bathherb" consist of the following well-known natural bathing preparations which have been handed down from ancient times: *Touki*[42] (for better circulation), *Senkyu*[43] (to relieve pain), *Hamaboufu*[44] (for better circulation), *Chinpi*[45] (to prevent a chill after the bath; for more beautiful skin), *Hakka*[46] (to expand the capillary vessels), and *Kamitsure*[47] (for better circulation). "BATHCRIN Bathherb" is the best bathing additive available, with the extracts of these natural medicines. It warms the body thoroughly, increases the blood flow, and stimulates metabolism. Therefore, it is effective for neuralgia, rheumatism, lumbago, shoulder stiffness, oversensitivity to cold, recovery from fatigue, hemorrhoids, pimples, chapped skin, eczema and heat rash.

Chapter IV
PAINTINGS

Woman and the bath is a fascinating subject for the artist. Among European masterpieces are splendid works dealing with the bath, including a painting by Renoir. This suggests that bathing creates or enhances female beauty.

Chatting with friends, relaxed and cheerful; combing the hair after bathing; concentration while applying make-up; absent of thought; physically radiant: for the artists the expressions and poses of women at the bath form a kaleidoscope of female beauty. The aesthetic expression of a painter can capture even the working of the model's mind. Here we present a collection of renowned paintings by well-known Japanese painters which address the bath and bathing. Admiring these portrayals of lovely women after bathing, we can reflect on bathing and the female charm it brings out.

The names of artists are given with the family name preceeding the given name.

1. *Ideyu* (Hot Spring), 1919.

by *Kobayashi Kokei* [48]

The artist's gaze is fixed on the woman in the bathtub. Kokei's realism is based in the realistic tradition of Japanese painting. This work is an objective portrayal of the woman's restful feeling, which we can sense in the neatness of the depiction and in her posture.

2. *Kami* (Hair), 1932.

by *Kobayashi Kokei*

This work, done with a modern sensibility, is in the highest realm of neo-classical art. The artist draws the clearly defined outline beautifully in India ink. Although this is the portrayal of a routine activity, combing the hair after the bath, he concentrates his attention on grasping her pure beauty and thus transforms a commonplace sight into art. This is a work which shows Kokei's deep understanding of classical art, and he breaks new ground for Japanese painting in the history of modern art.

3. *Yuna* (Woman Just After a Bath), 1918.

by *Tsuchida Bakusen*[49]

Bakusen always pursues the new and stimulating, and in this respect "Yuna" is one of his best works. It displays sophisticated and well-considered composition, the bright colors unique to Japanese painting, a keen modern sense, and the gorgeous but somehow pathetic mood of the public bath in his era. Combining these elements with a visionary image, Bakusen portrays a beautiful, and sensual woman fresh from the bath.
(Owned by The National Museum of Modern Art, Tokyo)

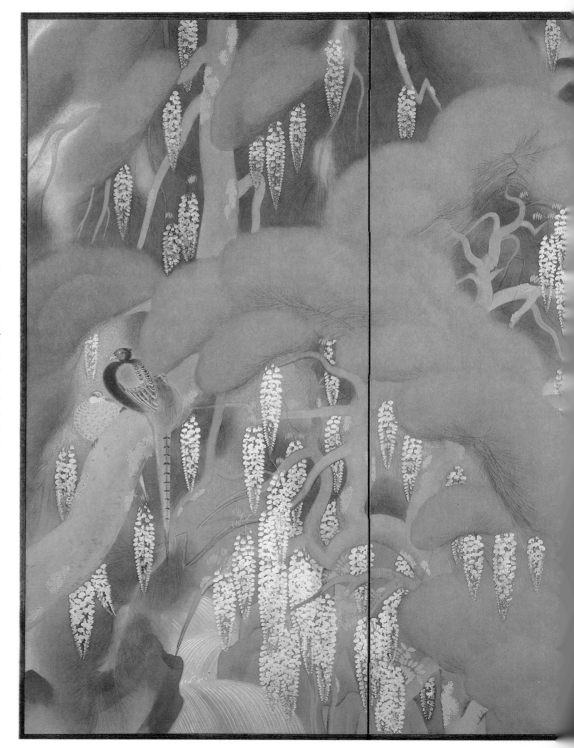

4. *Yokushitsu* (Bathroom), 1964.

by *Takayama Tatsuo*[50]

Takayama painted only female nudes in this period. Among the works he produced this is the finest piece, and it won the highest honors at the *Nitten* Exhibition. In the bathroom, two women are carefully washing their hair. This kind of portrayal shows the universal beauty of bathing women around the world. Takayama commented that the use of this skin tone occurred to him by chance while he was hanging on a strap in a train in a blank state of mind.

5. *Yokujo Sono-ichi* (Bathing Woman No.1), 1938.

by *Ogura Yuki* [51]

Two women are having a comfortable bath in a white-tiled bathtub. This is quite unique for the composition of the pose of the bather in the foreground; Yuki observes her Japanese coiffure from behind and her figure from above. She successfully depicts the beautiful balance of women and water in the small bathtub.

6. *Yokujo Sono-ni* (Bathing Woman No. 2),1939.

by *Ogura Yuki*

This work incisively captures an aspect of daily life. The patterned rattan mat gives a strong sense of depth to the painting. We see three women, one about to take a bath, another combing her hair after the bath, and the last having a cigarette and ready to go out. The composition of the work is ingenious and the artist depicts the women with vivid colors. With this piece we catch a glimpse of bath life.

7. *Dojo Nyuyokuno Zu* (Little girls taking bath), 1925.

by *Ogura Yuki*

This piece must evoke strong memories in the artist. She took it along on her visit to the well-known painter *Yasuda Yukihiko,* after which he accepted her as his pupil. This work also gained her the recognition of *Kobayashi Kokei.* Painted while she was teaching poor children in Kyoto, it reflects her deep affection for children. This is heartwarming painting.

8. *Joushin* (Clean Time), 1930.

by *Ito Shinsui* [52]

Shinsui here portrays five nude women taking an open-air bath at Shiobara hot spring resort. Clouds of white steam dim the scene. Among the murmuring of the stream and the singing birds in the quiet valley, they enjoy their bath while chattering amongst themselves. Their cheerful voices almost echo to us. This is probably one of the most beautiful sights of Japan.
(Owned by Meguro Gajoen)

9. *Yuami* (Bathing), 1946.

by *Hirota Tatsu*[53]

A mother gives her child a bath, which is a happy sight common to all places. She watches the child with eyes full of attection. The child places complete reliance on her and plays the baby to her. Only artists who are themselves mothers are capable of producing this kind of work.

(Photo: by courtesy of Shueisha Co., Ltd)

10. *Yuno Yado* (Japanese hot spring Inn), 1913.

by *Imamura Shiko*[54]

Steam is rising from a hot spring bath. This is a work which appears to be an India ink drawing, but the bathhouse and trees are drawn in the *Nanga* style (the southern school of Chinese painting). Shiko depicts the details scrupulously. This is the only work in which he tried a double-sided vignette technique, and it reproduces the moist atmosphere with good effect.
(Owned by Yokohama Museum of Art)

11. *Ideyu No Ame* (Rain in a Hot Spring), 1931.

by *Kajiwara Hisako*[55]

This is a depiction of a scene at a simple hot spring resort, where spring is slow in coming amid the surrounding mountains. Steam mixed with rain enhances the creation of the hot spring mood further. A young woman who appears to be a guest stands in front of a bathhouse. She is holding an umbrella, the colors of which provide a slight accent to the overall dark tone of the painting. Hisako painted this when she visited Shirahone hot spring in Shinshu, and she herself was the model. This is a scene rich in the atmosphere of Japan's "good old days."
(Owned by Kyoto Municipal Museum of Art)

12. *Yuami Shite* (After the Bath), 1975.

by *Nakamura Teiji* [56]

Nude to the waist, a young woman is examining her hair in a mirror after her bath. The artist observes from behind and draws her body with strong, elegant and steady lines. The softness of her skin is revealed by the refined taste of these lines. This painting is full of the refreshment and ease which follow the bath. The unique beauty of woman shines out in such artistic expressions as this work.

(Photo: by courtesy of Shueisha Co., Ltd)

13. *Yuagari* (After the Bath), middle of Showa era.

by *Kobayakawa Kiyoshi* [57]

The artist portrays a woman with freshly washed hair after her bath. Although there is no mirror in the picture, she is sitting in front of her dresser and about to start applying her makeup after the bath. She turns back a little to the artist with a stern and uncanny look in her eye. After the bath, women often appear a little unusual and uncanny.

(Photo: by courtesy of Shueisha Co., Ltd)

14. *Yokushitsu* (Bathroom), 1933.

by *Ochiai Rofu*[58]

A generously proportioned young woman is combing her hair in a tiled bathroom. The bathtub is full of warm water. Sitting on her heels in the traditional manner, in the modern bathroom, she forms an interesting contrast of East and West which might symbolize the situation of the bath in contemporary Japan.

(Owned by The National Museum of Modern Art, Tokyo)

15. *Shoubuyu* (Sweet Flag Bath), date unknown.

by *Kaburagi Kiyokata*[59]

An essay entitled "Sweet Flag Bath," written in April of Showa 9 (1934), mentions a concubine taking a bath at midday. This painting likely is from the same era. A sweet flag bath has leaves and roots of the sweet flag in its warm water and is said to ward off malice from the bather. Furthermore, the Japanese have long been fond of such baths for their effectiveness in warming the body and for their delightful seasonal fragrance. (Owned by Matsuoka Museum of Art)

16. *Mushiburo* (Steam Bath).

by *Sawa Kojin*[60]

Mother and child bathing in a *teppo-buro,* a traditional bath of the Kohoku area. The artist made the following comments about this work: "I guess this bath is a kind ot *teppo-buro.* They were used in the Kohoku area in the old days. The title 'Mushiburo' (steamy bath) was chosen for no particular reason." The corn and red peppers hanging from a beam, and beanstalks and pods lying around, give a simple and warm feeling to this work. (Owned by The Museum of Modern Art, Shiga)

Chapter V
UKIYOE

Ukiyoe is a style of expression which emerged during the Edo era. Using brushes or wood-block printing techniques, ukiyoe artists addressed the customs, manners and preferences of the day in works which have been classified according to subject matter: beautiful women, actors, landscapes, and erotica. It is generally considered that ukiyoe first appeared around 1681 and enjoyed a golden age lasting until the end of the nineteenth century, being well accepted by the common people. Ukiyoe was introduced to Europe at the end of the Edo era, where the style immediately developed a following. The influence of these works has been widely acknowledged as a factor in the emergence of new styles of European art such as impressionism.

Out of the many remaining ukiyoe works, those centering on the subjects of the bath and bathing women have been selected for inclusion here. These depictions of bath life and the lifestyle of the Japanese during the Edo and Meiji eras obviously suggest that their subjects enjoyed a profound fondness of bathing. Creating an impression distinctly different from the *Nihon-ga* works which also appear in these pages, ukiyoe offer us a vivid portrayal of everyday life with a very realistic touch.

Since ukiyoe images which relate to the theme of bathing are taken up here, not a few of them incorporate rather erotic overtones, and the sensual images of women after bathing and the realistic approach reflect an essence of ukiyoe. At the same time, works of ukiyoe perform valuable service in terms of historical references because they accurately depict the life of their times, such as the prostitutes of the *Yoshiwara*[61] licensed quarter, the public baths and the floating baths on boats. These scenes are curious and intriguing to we contemporary Japanese.

While *Utamaro, Hiroshige* and *Hokusai*[62] are widely known ukiyoe artists, works of lesser-known talents are reproduced here as well thanks to the assistance of *Kazuhiko Fukuda,* a well-known authority on ukiyoe and paintings of the female nude.

The names of artists are given with the family name preceeding the given name.

1. Portable Bathtub and Pail

Made at the close of the 16th century in the Momoyama era, these belonged to *Kitamandokoro*[63], the mother of *Toyotomi Hideyoshi*[64]. The bathtub is on the right, the pail on the left; both are lacquered with a paulownia pattern which was the family crest of the Toyotomis. Formerly used while traveling, they are now kept by the Ashimori family in Ashimori, Okayama Prefecture.

2. Beauty Painting after the Bath (*Yuagari Bijin-ga* from *Seirou Nanakomachi, Ogiya-nai Takigawa*)
by *Kitagawa Utamaro*[65]

Onishiki size[66], Izumisa version. Printed in the Kansai Period (1789-1800)

A large portrait of the licensed prostitute Takigawa of the Ogiya house of the *Shin-Yoshiward*[67] district depicting the chic beauty of her clear skin with her hair in a snail chignon after the bath.

157

3. Beauty Painting after the Bath (*Yuagari Bijin-ga* from *Yoshiwaratokei Minokoku, Hiru Yotsu*)
   by *Utagawa Kunisada*[68]

Onishiki size. Printed in the Bunsei Period (1818-1829)

A licensed resident of Shin-Yoshiwara after her bath. The white pattern of water birds on a blue ground suits her light summer *kimono* perfectly. Through the window frame in the background we observe employees having an early supper.

4. Beauty Painting after the Bath (*Yuagari Bijin-ga* from *Ukiyo Juroku Musashi*) by *Utagawa Kunisada.*

Onishiki size. Printed in the Bunsei Period (1818-1829)

A *geisha* after her bath on a hot summer day. She may have a meal after bathing; *soba* (buckwheat noodles) and a cool broth in which to dip them are behind her.

159

5. Genre Picture in Public Bathhouse (*Kyoudouburo, Sento Fuuzoku Zu* from *Higozuiki Shohen*)
by *Keisai Eisen*[69]

Printed in the Bunsei Period (1818-1829)

The women's bathroom of a public bathhouse, showing the washing area. On the right is a tub from which warm water is ladled into small tubs for use in washing. This tub is for ladling only; for soaking and warming the body another tub in the rear was used.

6. Bathing Beauty in Portable Bathtub (*Gyouzui Bijin* from *Soushi Araikomachi*) by *Utagawa Toyokuni* [70] (former *Utagawa Kunisada*)

Onishiki size. Printed in Kaei 1 (1853)

In the heat of summer, women would bath using portable bathtubs once a day. After filling the tub with warm water, they would dip a towel in the tub and with it wipe the perspiration from their bodies. This is a really slmple bath.

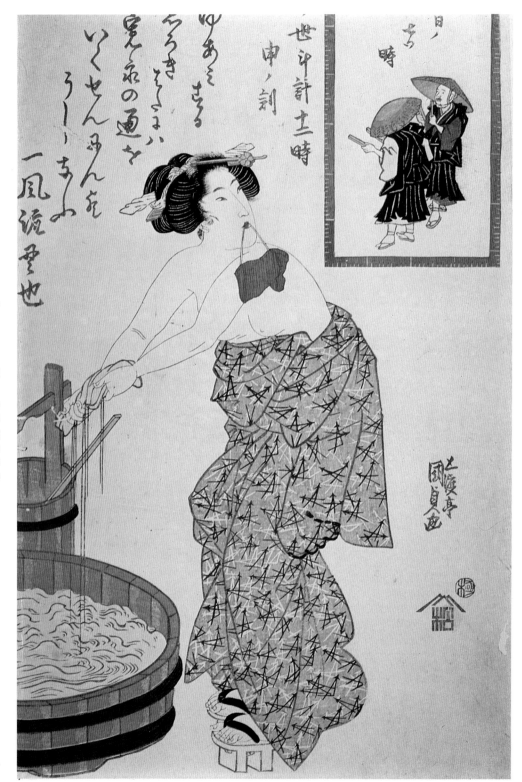

7. Bathing Beauty in Portable Bathtub
   (*Gyouzui Bijin* from *Ukiyotokei Juniji,*
   Sarunokoku)
   by *Utagawa Kunisada*

Onishiki size. Printed in the Bunsei Period
(1818-1829)

   A woman bathes in midsummer using a
large portable bathtub full of warm water. In
her mouth she holds a red pouch containing
rice hulls—in the absence of soap in those
days, the rice hulls which were a by-product
of the rice polishing process were used to
clean the body.

8. Bathing Beauty in Portable Bathtub
   (*Gyouzui Bijin*)
   by *Utagawa Toyokuni*

On a hot summer day a woman bathes outdoors with her portable bathtub. Behind her
is a crape myrtle, whose red flowers bloom in
summer and are a seasonal sight in Japan.

9. Sweet Flag Bath (Series of Two Pieces)
   (*Shoubuyu*)
   by *Utagawa Kunisada*

Onishiki size. Printed in the Bunsei Period
(1818-1829)

On May 5, the day of the traditional Boy's
Festival, Japanese bathe in water to which
sweet flag leaves have been added even today. At the close of the 16th century, prostitutes began taking such sweet flag baths every
day, as shown in these prints of a bathroom
in the Shin-Yoshiwara licensed quarters. A
sweet flag bath warms the body well and,
because of its strong fragrance, was used by
these women to keep themselves neat.

10. Beautiful Woman Washing Hair (*Kamiarai Bijin* from
Oatsurae Tousegonomi)
by *Utagawa Kunisada*

Onishiki size. Printed in the Bunsei Period (1818-1829)
   Wearing a light summer *kimono* of Oshima pongee, a woman
is combing her hair after washing it. Camellia oil, extracted from
camellia seeds, was used in those days as hair oil.

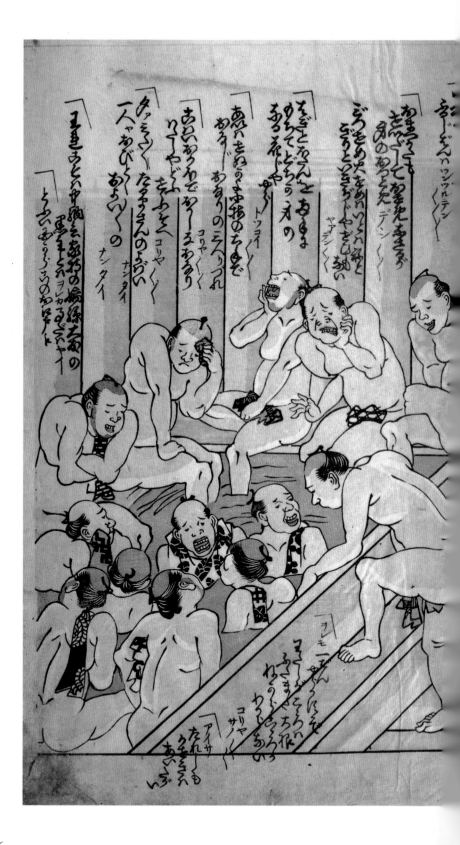

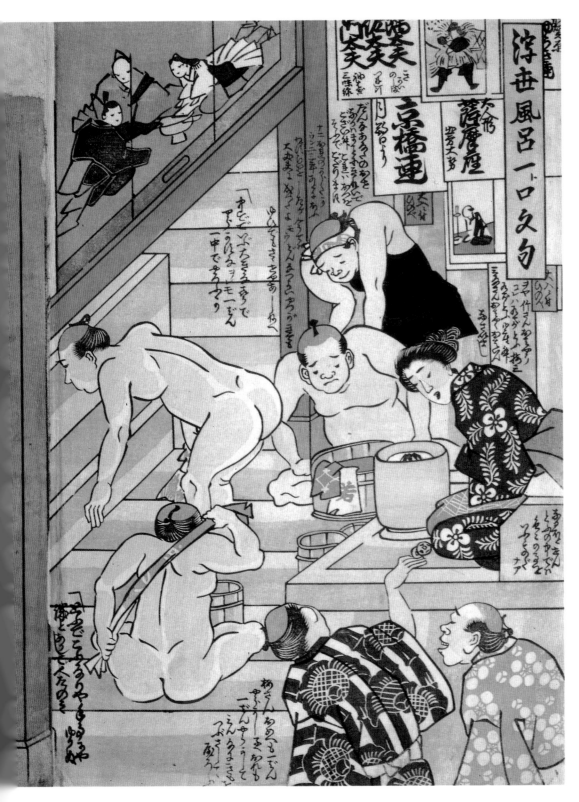

11. Public Bath (Series of Two Pieces)
(*Ukiyoburo* from *Ukiyoburo Hitokuchi-monku*)
by *Utagawa Hiroshige*[71] (later *Ando Hiroshige*)

Onishiki size. Printed in Kaei 4 (1851)

A men's bathroom at a public bath. On the right, a woman is sitting on the *bandai* platform to collect payment from the customers. The washing space is located just beyond, and the bathroom has a *zakuro-guchi* ("pomegranate entrance") to the left of the *bandai*, consisting of a shutter-board which hangs from the ceiling half-way to the floor which bathers must duck to enter the bath area. The *zakuro-guchi* was designed to retain heat within the bath area. The men in the tub are having a lively chat.

12. Public Bath (Series of Two Pieces)
(*Ukiyoburo* from *Ukiyoburo Hitokuchi-
monku*)
by *Utagawa Hiroshige*

A women's bathroom. On the right is the
bathtub area with its *zakuro-guchi*. This bathroom has a large washing area—these washing areas for women were twice as large or
more than the men's washing areas in the
Edo era. The bath fee was a little higher for
women than for men, of course.

13. Genre Picture in Women's Bath-room of Public Bathhouse (*Onnayu Fuzokuzu* from *Imayou-nenju-gyouji-no-uchi*)
by *Utagawa Yoshiiku*[72]

Onishiki size. Printed in Keio 2 (1866)
    A quarrel among women in the washing area of a public bath heats up to the point of brandishing a wooden bucket. Such fights were everyday affairs in the bathhouses of the era.

14. Steam Bath (*Mushiburo* from *Sento Shinwa*)
by *Utagawa Kunisada*

Printed in the Bunsei Period (1818-1829) .

At the beginning of the 19th century another type of public bath was added to the existing warm water baths: the steam bath. They were known as *irikomi* ("push-in bathhouses") due to their mixed bathing system. The print shows a man in the steam bath who tries to seduce a fellow bather. "It's sure hot in here. This is a nice steam bath, isn't it?"

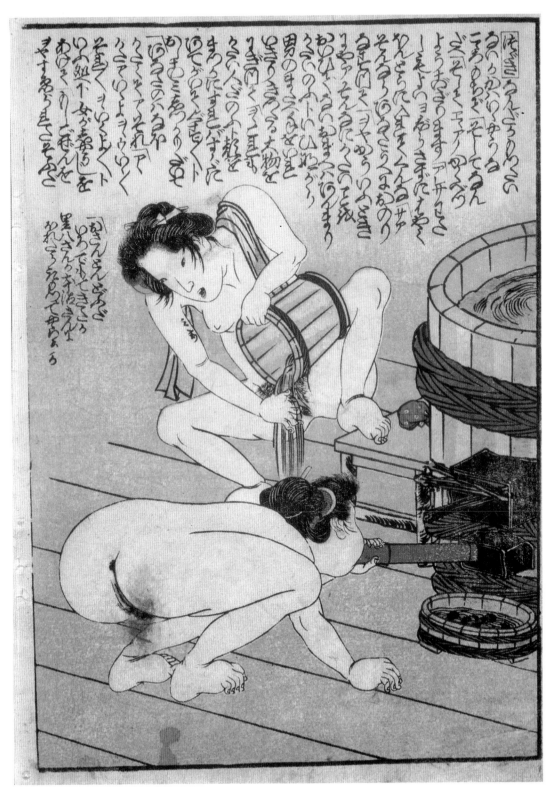

15. Bath Making (*Furo-taki* from *Sento Shinwa*)
by *Utagawa Kunisada*

Ordinary people were prohibited from having bathing facilities in their own homes during the Edo era. This print depicts a bath in the Shin-Yoshiwara licensed quarters, where a maid is making a fire for the bath.

16. Bathing in Portable Bathtub on Summer Day (*Natsuno-hino-Gyouzui* from *Kaichu Nenju Gyouji*)
by *Keisai Eisen*

Printed in Tenpo 5 (1834)
   Toward evening, this woman doesn't visit a public bath but rather takes her portable tub outdoors for her bath. This style of bathing was popular at most houses in the summer.

17. Painting of Beauties in Women's Bathroom (*Onna-yu-no Bijinga*
    from *Higo Zuiki*)
    by *Keisai Eisen*

Printed in the Bunsei period (1818-1829)
  Three beautiful women bathing. Their postures reflect the freedom of
the public bathhouse, and the artist depicts the beauty of their unhampered
bodies and limbs.

18. Bath in Boat (*Senchu-buro* from *Sento Shinwa*)
   by *Utagawa Kunisada*

From the close of the 18th century to the beginning of the 19th century, bathboats were tremendously popular in Edo. Customers from the monied classes took great enjoyment in the other-worldly experience of bathing in a boat floating on a river. They drank quantities of sake, womanized, and generally had a delightfully decadent time.

NOTES

Chapter I

THE TRENDY BATH LIFE

1 Shuji Miura
Shuji C, Miura Atelier
Tel. 03-3589-1100
5-7 5F, Azabudai, 3-chome Minato-ku, Tokyo 106
Designed the Nunoi residence

2 Alvin Toffler
American futurologist. Born in 1928 in New York. Graduate of New York University. Former vice editor of Fortune Magazine, former visiting professor at Cornell University, advisor to the Rockefeller Foundation. Author of "Future Shock", "The Third Wave", etc.

3 Pittori Piccoli
Pittori Piccoli Inc.
Tel. 03-3306-2933
3-9-16, Sakurajosui, Setagaya-ku, Tokyo 156
Designed the Shimono residence.

4 Junji Kawada
Born December 12, 1951 in Tokyo. Graduated from Tokyo National University of Fine Arts and Music in 1975. Graduated from Graduate School of above in 1977. Joined Takamitsu Azuma Architect & Associates in 1977. Established Junji Kawada Architect & Associates in 1981.
Junji Kawada Architect & Associates
Tel. 03-3499-8296
304 New Aoyama Bldg.,1-4-6, Shibuya, Shibuya-ku, Tokyo 150
Designed the Yano residence.

5 Masako Hayashi
Born July 11, 1928 in Hokkaido. Graduated from Japan Women's University. Established Hayashi, Yamada, Nakahara Architects in 1983. Designs residences using traditional Japanese techniques for arranging space. Received a prize from the Architectural Institute of Japan in 1981. She is one of the greatest Japanese architects.
Hayashi, Yamada, Nakahara Architects
Tel. 03-3353-2275
19, Minami-Motomachi, Shinjuku-ku, Tokyo 160
Designed the Suzuki residence.

6 Ushida Findlay Partnership
Tel. 03-3440-4609
5-12-15-402, Kitashinagawa, Shinagawa-ku, Tokyo 141
Designed Echo Timber

7 Minami House Design and Construction Co., Ltd.
Designer; Takashi Nishidate
Tel. 03-3308-2620
5-24-7, Minami-Karasuyama, Setagaya-ku, Tokyo 157
Designed the Ukita residence

8 Manami Fuji
Actress. Born January, 1938 in Mishima Shizuoka Prefecture. Graduated from Mishima Kita High School. Debuted in 1957, and has always been a popular actress.
Today she is active as a writer in addition to her acting work.

9 Yukiko Hanai
Fashion designer. Born November 12, 1937 in Kanagawa Prefecture. Graduated from Tama High School in 1956. Started Atelier Hanai in 1964, after working with Ad Center. Established Madame Hanai in 1971. Since then, she has always been a leading fashion designer.

10 Eizo Shiina
Architect. Born in 1945 in Tokyo. Graduated from Nippon University in 1967. Established Eizo Shiina Architect & Associates in 1976.
Eizo Shiina Architect & Associates
Tel. 03-3405-9195
1-15-22-103, Minami-Aoyama, Minato-ku, Tokyo 107
Designed the Hanai residence.

11 Yoshinobu Ashihara
Architect. Born July 7, 1918 in Tokyo. Graduated from Tokyo University in 1942. Graduated from Harvard University Graduate School in 1953. Established Ashihara Architect & Associates in 1956. Received a prize from the Architectural Institute of Japan for the design of the Chuo-Koron Building. Since then he has designed various kinds of buildings, and is now one of Japan's leading architects.
Ashihara Architect & Associates
Tel: 03-3405-9151
103 Villa Nogizaka
1-15-22, Minami-Aoyama, Minato-ku, Tokyo 107
Designed the residence of Mr. Wilks and Dr. Precker

12 whirlpool
Rounded bath tub in which jets of warm water form small whirlpools. Effective in massaging the entire body.

13 Pension Alm
Tel. 0266-77-2765
6044-6, Chuo-Kogen, Kitayama-Tateshina, Chino-City
Nagano Prefecture 391-03

14 Kurhaus
"Kur" means to cure or to take a rest for one's health in German. It has a history of nearly 300 years in Germany, its birthplace, where more than 50 million people use Kurhauses every year. Recently, Kurhauses which feature training rooms and sports facilities have become popular in Japan. Kurhauses offer facilities and programs which are ideal for the promotion of health and furthermore provide opportunities to enjoy leisure and sightseeing.

15 Southern Cross Resort
Tel. 0557-45-1234
1006-1, Yoshida, Ito-City, Shizuoka Prefecture 414
Tel: 03-3595-2551
1F., No. 5 Mori Bldg., 1-17-1, Toranomon, Minato-ku, Tokyo 150

16 Mer Club
Tel: 0558-62-3672
112, Shimokamo, Minami-Izumachi, Kamo-gun, Shizuoka Prefecture 415-03

17 utase-yu
A bath in which stiff, sore parts of the body are placed directly under falling hot water. The heat and pressure of the hot water improve blood circulation and ease muscle stiffness with a vigorous massaging effect.

18 ne-yu
A bath which permits bathing by lying and relaxing in warm water at a moderate temperature in a shallow bath tub. This helps relieve stress as blood vessels near skin are gradually dilated and blood circulation is improved, and also has a tranquilizing and hypnotizing effect.

19 Spatz
Tel. 03-3404-0822
18-11, Shinsen-cho, Shibuya-ku, Tokyo 150

20 Andree Putman
Interior designer. Born in Paris. Worked as a musician and journalist before becoming a designer. Won high praise for the interior design of the Hotel Morgan. His works include designs for Yve Saint Laurent boutiques, the VIP room of the 1989 Paris Summit, and the library of President Mitterand. Luxurious color and ultra-modern designs characterize his work.

21 Le Lac
Tel. 0555-73-3309
1219, Kodachi, Kawaguchiko-machi, Minami-Tsuru-gun, Yamanashi Prefecture 401-03

22 Yagyu No Sho
Tel. 0558-72-4126
1116-6, Shuzenji, Shuzenji-cho, Tagata-gun, Shizuoka Prefecture 410-24

23 Okada Architectural Office
Tetsuro Okada Architectural Office
Tel. 03-3408-4417
2-7-2, Minami-Aoyama, Minato-ku, Tokyo 107
Designed Yagyu No Sho

24 shoin
A style of architecture employed for *samurai* residences. In the beginning, it was used for places to read or to give lectures in a temple, but later was used for living rooms or studies in the homes of *samurai* or court nobles.

25 sukiya
A tea-ceremony room separated from the main building, reportedly originated by *Shuko Murata* in the Muromachi era. It appeared in the 16th century and became popular among all classes. This style of tea-ceremony room was used in residences, the villas of *daimyo* and nobles, and in teahouse restaurants.

26 Taiseikan
Tel. 0460-2-2281
72, Miyanoshita, Hakone-machi, Ashigarashimo-gun
Kanagawa Prefecture 240-02

27 Shu Uemura Esthetic Salon
Tel. 03-3486-7578
5-7-5, Jingumae, Shibuya-ku, Tokyo 150

Chapter II

A HISTORY OF THE JAPANEASE BATH

28 Dogo
Located in the east of Matsuyama City, Ehime Prefecture, Dogo is said to be the oldest spa in Japan It is a simple spa with a rich literary atmosphere as it was visited by many writers and poets.

29 Arima
Located at the foot of Mt. Rokko in Kobe City, Hyogo Prefecture, it is said to be one of the oldest spas in Japan together with Kusatsu and Dogo. It has a long history highlighted by visits of the imperial family, high priests and generals from ancient times.

30 Basil Hall Chamberlain
English Japanologist (October 18, 1850–February 15, 1935) The son of a naval officer from Portsmouth, Chamberlain came to Japan in 1873 and acquired a thorough knowledge of classical Japanese literature. He taught at the naval academy, and taught linguistics and Japanese in Tokyo University's Literature Department. After leaving Japan in 1911, he introduced Japanese literature to the world by translating it.

31 Kunio Yanagida
Folklorist, authority on agricultural administration, poet. (June 31, 1875–August 8, 1962) Born in Hyogo Prefecture, he graduated from Tokyo Imperial University and then served as a secretary at the House of Peers, and was later employed by the Asahi Shimbun Publishing Company. He devoted his private life to researching folklore, and established the Institute of Folklore. Awarded an Order of Cultural Merit. "Tono Stories" is his masterpiece.

32 Thyunzyoubou Tyougen
A Buddist priest of the Jodo sect in the Kamakura era. When *Todaiji* Temple burned down in the 14th year of the Jisho era, he was appointed *Daikanjin* (construction manager for the rebuilding of the temple). He was a typical priest of the Kamakura era who devoted himself to social welfare activities, such as building bridges and seeking pardons for condemned criminals.

33 Garan
A building in a temple where Buddist monks live and practice asceticism.

34 Yase
"Furusato" (Yase's Kamaburo, today)
Tel. 075-791-4126
239, Yasekonoe-cho, Sakyo-ku, Kyoto-City, Kyoto 601-12

35 Minamotono Yoritomo
1147–1199. The first *shogun* of the Kamakura Shogunate, he took control of the country by destroying the *Heike* clan in the battles of Ichinotani and Dannoura. Although he established the Kamakura Shogunate, power shifted to the *Hojo* family after his death because he had killed many of his kin and vassals.

36 Hojo Masako (Tairano Masako)
Wife of *Minamotono Yoritomo* and mother of *Yoriie* and *Sanetomo*, she became a nun after *Yoritomo*'s death. After the death of her son *Sanetomo*, she brought *Fujiwarano Yoritsune* from Kyoto to make him *Shogun* and governed the Shogunate in his shadow.

37 Akechi Mitsuhide
1526–1582. Served *Oda Nobunaga,* and later attacked his master at *Honnoji* Temple, driving *Nobunaga* to suicide. In only 13 days, he was defeated by *Toyotomi Hideyoshi* and killed by farmers at Ogurusu.

38 kakari-yu
Pouring hot water over the body to prepare it for the bath. By doing this, blood vessels are dilated so that dizziness caused by the rapid increase of blood pressure can be avoided.

39 Kano Tanyu
Artist of the early Edo era. (1602–1674). He later named himself *Tanyusai*. As an artist with wide variety of skills in painting, he was patronized by the *Tokugawa* Shogunate and led his clan to prosperity. The wall paintings on *fusuma* screens at *Nijo* Castle and *Nagoya* Castle are among his numerous works.

40 Santo Kyoden
Author of popular stories. (1761–1816). Born *Iwase Samuru,* and popularly known as *Denzo*. His pen name *"Kyoden"* derives from his nickname and means "*Denzo* living in Kyobashi" After publishing many *Kibyoshi* and *Yomihon* (popular books of stories), he was condemned to be handcuffed for 50 days on charges of corrupting the morals of the public in the third year of the Kanei era.

41 Daikoku-yu
  Tel. 03-3882-4646
  32-6, Senju Kotobuki-cho, Adachi-ku, Tokyo 120

Chapter III

THE EFFICACY OF BATHING

42 Touki
  This is a perennial herb belonging to the Umbelliferae family, and will grow anywhere. It is used for pain, sedation, to alleviate fever, and for irregular menstruation.

43 Senkyu
  This plant was introduced from China, and is a perennial member of the Umbelliferae family which grows anywhere. Its roots and rhizomes are antithrombic and promote hematogenesis, making it suitable for the treatment of anemia, poor circulation, irregular menstruation, female disorders and so on.

44 Hamaboufu
  Growing wild in coastal districts, this herb also belongs to the Umbelliferae family. The roots and rhizomes of this plant are good for arthralgia, headaches, pains, dizziness, and cramps in the hands and legs.

45 Chinpi
  The peel of a ripe fruit of the Rutacceae family, it suppresses stomach aches, vomiting, coughs and phlegm.

46 Hakka
  A perennial member of the Labiatae family which grows anywhere, it refreshes the mouth and is good for lacquer poisoning when applied externally. It is also efficacious for sweating, fevers, and the common cold.

47 Kamitsure
  Roman camomile and German camomile grow in Europe, where they have long been used for medicinal purposes. They commonly grow in unused plots in the south of England and Wales, where they are called the "scented weeds of May" and are taken as camomile tea. They are used for bath liquids, and the sweating and moisturizing they promote makes them good for poor circulation, neuralgia, rheumatism and other ailments.

Chapter IV

PAINTINGS

48 Kobayashi Kokei
  Nihonga (Japanese-style) painter. (February 11, 1883–April 3, 1957). Born *Kobayashi Shigeru* in Niigata Prefecture. Displayed talent even in his childhood, later studied Nihonga painting. Awarded many prizes for paintings of historical scenes before creating masterpieces such a "Ideyu" (hot spring), "Itan" (paganism), and others. Became prominent with the exhibition of "Kami" (the long black hair of a woman). Awarded Order of Cultural Merit in 1950. The New Classical Style that Kokei mastered indicated a new way of Japanese painting.

49 Tsuchida Bakusen
  Nihonga painter. (February 9, 1887–June 10, 1936). Born *Tsuchida Kinji* at Sado Island, Niigata Prefecture. Graduated from Kyoto-shiritsu Kaiga Senmon Gakko (Kyoto municipal college of art) in 1911. Awarded Third Prize at the second Bunten (the national exhibition under the auspices of the Department of Education) in 1908 for "Batsu" (punishment). Awarded Third Prize at the 1915 Bunten for "Oharame" (a female vendor in Ohara, Kyoto). Resigned from Bunten and founded the Kokuga Sosaku Kyokai (national paintings creation society) in 1918. Travelled in Europe in 1921, returned to Japan in 1923. Incorporating ideas from Western painting, he created tightly organized space in his works, and painted a series of brilliantly colored *maiko* (apprentice *geisha*).

50 Takayama Tatsuo
  Nihonga painter. Born June 26, 1912 in Oita City, Oita Prefecture. Graduated from Tokyo School of Art (presently Tokyo National University of Fine Arts and Music) in 1936, and became a professional artist. First admitted to the 15th Teiten (Imperial Academy Art Exhibition) in 1934 for "Yusen" (hot spring). Awarded Tokusen Prize (highest honors) at Nitten (the art exhibition sponsored by the Juridical Corporate Association) for "Yokushitsu" (bathroom) and "Shojo" (a young girl), and received many other prizes. Awarded Order of Cultural Merit in 1982. Takayama has created many excellent portraits, which are said to be manifestations of his sincere quest for humanity.

51 Ogura Yuki
Nihonga painter. Born March 1, 1895 in Otsu City, Shiga Prefecture. Graduated from Nara Women's Senior High School in 1917. Became a teacher at Soshin Women's School in 1920 and began to study Nihonga painting under *Yasuda Yukihiko,* in the same year. Awarded the Uemura Shoen Prize for "O-fujin Zazo" (seated figure of Mrs. O) in 1954. Awarded the Mainichi Fine Art Prize for "Shojo" (a little girl) in 1957. Awarded Order of Cultural Merit in 1980. Took office as Chairman of the Board of the Nihon Bijutsuin (Japan Art Institute) in 1990.

52 Ito Shinsui
Nihonga painter. (February 4, 1898–May 8, 1972). Born *Ito Hajime* in Tokyo. Studied Nihonga painting under the instruction of *Nakayama Shuko,* beginning in 1908. Began studying with *Kaburagi Kiyokata* in 1911. First admitted to Saiko Nihon Bijutsuin Ten (Reorganized Japan Art Institute Exhibition) for "Sajiki no Onna" (a woman sitting in a box seat at the theater) in 1914, and to the Bunten in 1915 for "Juroku-no Onna" (a girl of sixteen years). Afterwards, participated in the new print movement, as well as drawing frontispieces and illustrations for books. Established Shinsui Art School in 1927. Became a member of the Nihon Geijutsuin (Japan Art Academy) in 1958. Working as a contemporary Ukiyoe artist, a witness of the age, he portrayed healthy women.

53 Hirota Tatsu
Nihonga painter. Born May 10, 1904 in Kyoto. Graduated from Takiike Primary School in 1916. Determined to become a Nihonga painter around the year 1919. First admitted to the Bunten for "Akibare" (blue autumn sky) in 1936. Afterwards, exhibited at the Shin Bunten, Nitten, and Shinseisakuten. Awarded Tokusen Prize at the second Nitten for "Yuami" (bathing). Became principal of Kyoto Nihonga Senmon Gakko in 1977.

54 Imamura Shiko
Nihonga painter. Born *Imamura Jusaburo* in Yokohama Kanagawa Prefecture in 1880. Decided to become a Nihonga painter at the age of 15. Took the name *Imamura Shiko* in 1898, when first admitted to the Nihon Bijutsu Kyokai Ten (Japan Fine Art Association Exhibition). His work is characterized by the use of brilliant colors.

55 Kajiwara Hisako
Nihonga painter. Born *Kajiwara Hisa* on December 22, 1896. Graduated from Second Kyoto Municipal Women's Senior High School in 1914. Awarded the Sengai Kasaku (honorable mention) at the first Kokuga Sousaku Kyokai Ten (National Paintings Creation Society Exhibition) for "Kureyuku Teiryujo" (bus stop in the late afternoon) in 1918. Has exhibited many works since then, and has participated in the Teiten. Awarded the Tokusho (highest honorable prize) at the third Nitten Exhibition for "Banryo" (enjoy the cool of the evening) in 1947. Exhibited "Ideyu no Ame" (rain in a hot spring) at the second Teiten in 1931.

56 Nakamura Teiji
Nihonga painter. (July 23, 1900–March 12, 1982). Born *Nakamura Kiyosada* in Osaka. Began to study under *Hasegawa Sadanobu,* Ukiyoe artist, in 1909. First admitted to the Nihon Bijutsuin Shisaku Ten (The Japan Art Institute Trial Exhibition) for "Sennyo" (the nymph) in 1923, drawing praise from *Yokoyama Taikan.* Awarded the Insho (Japan Art Institute Prize) for "Asa" (the morning) in 1932. Later exhibited many fine works for which his eldest daughter modeled.

57 Kobayakawa Kiyoshi
Nihonga painter. (1897–1948). Became known through exhibitions under the auspices of the national government, and is known for his major works such as "Nagasaki no Okikusan" (Ms. Okiku of Nagasaki), "Rankan Fujo no Zu" (women in a Dutch trading firm's building in Nagasaki) and others. Studied under *Kaburagi Kiyokata,* and belonged to Seikinkai, a group of Bijinga (portraits of beautiful women) artists.

58 Ochiai Rofu
Born in Shiba, Tokyo. Studied at the Kawabata Fine Arts School. Exhibited at both the Bunten and the Teiten, as well as the Seiryu-ten and the In-ten. Resigned from the Seiryu-ten and established the Meiro Bijutsu Renmei (convivial fine art federation) in 1934. He was a Christian and died in his early years to the sorrow of his many fans.

59 Kaburagi Kiyokata
Nihonga painter. (August 31, 1878–March 2, 1972). Born *Kaburagi Kenichi* at Kanda, Tokyo. Began to study illustration under *Mizuno Toshikata,* an Ukiyoe portrait artist who specialized in depicting beautiful girls, in 1891 when he was 13 years old. Began drawing newspaper illustrations around 1894. His "Ichiyo Joshi no Haka" (the tomb of *Higuchi Ichiyo*), shown at the Ugou-kai Exhibition in 1902, attracted much attention, and his status was established when he exhibited "Sumidagawa Funa-asobi" (boat party on the Sumida River) in 1914. The next year, he was awarded the Tokusen at the Bunten for "Kurokami" (a girl with long black hair), and

he painted many other masterpieces during the following years. Awarded Order of Cultural Merit in 1954. His paintings portray the daily life of the common *Edokko* (Tokyoite) of his time.

60 Sawa Kojin
Nihonga painter. (March 18, 1905–September 24, 1982) Born *Sawa Hiroshi* in Shiga Prefecture. Graduated Kyoto-shiritsu Kaiga Senmon Gakko, later exhibited at governmental exhibitions. Participated in organizing Sozo Bijutsu Kyokai (Creative Fine Art Association). His main works include "Shayo" (the setting sun) from 1940, and "Yubae" (the sunset glow).

Chapter V

UKIYOE

61 Yoshiwara
District of Tokyo in premodern times, located near present-day Nihonbashi, Chuo-ku. Developed as the liscenced quarters for prostitutes since 1616 or thereabout.

62 Hokusai
Ukiyoe artist of the later Edo Period, originater of the Katsushika School of Ukiyoe woodblock prints. First apprenticed to *Katsukawa Shunsho,* he depicted *Kabuki* actors and beautiful women, and later produced many landscapes which incorporate techniques of Western art. His series of woodblock prints called "Thirty-Six Views of Mt. Fuji" is especially famous around the world.

63 Kitamandokoro
Generally speaking, this is the name of the rank held by the wife of a *Sessho* (regent) or *Kanpaku* (chief adviser to the emperor) who assumed the responsibilities of an emperor. Often used to refer to *Koudai-in Nene,* the wife of *Toyotomi Hideyoshi.*

64 Toyotomi Hideyoshi
(1536–1598) Warrior of the Sengoku and Azuchi-Momoyama Periods in Japan. At first subjected to *Oda Nobunaga,* he later unified the country by killing *Akechi Mitsuhide* in the *Honnoji no Hen* (the mutiny of *Akechi Mitsuhide* against *Oda Nobunaga*). He tried to conquer Ming dynasty China and had his troops invade Korea, but he died in Japan during the war.

65 Kitagawa Utamaro
Ukiyoe artist of the Edo Period. (1753?–1806). The details of his life are mostly unknown, including even his birth place. He studied drawing in his childhood, and produced his first work in 1775. He showed artistic talent in his early years with his pictures of flowers and birds. Around 1790 he started producing portraits of beautiful women, and his talents exceeded those of preceding artists who had also depicted the same subjects. His works which capture the moment of a woman's gesture are the highest masterpieces of Ukiyoe Bijinga (Ukiyoe portraits of beautiful women).

66 Onishiki size
Large, multi-colored Ukiyoe woodblock prints of about 27 cm by 39 cm.

67 Shin-Yoshiwara
A district of Tokyo in premodern times, located near Asakusa, Taito-ku. The Edo Shogunate decided in 1659 to move the old *Yoshiwara* community from central Tokyo to this district on the outskirts of the city to put the liscenced quarters at a distance from the central district.

68 Utagawa Kunisada
Ukiyoe artist of the later Edo Period. (1786–1864). Born in Edo (now called Tokyo), he served an apprenticeship with *Utagawa Toyokuni* to learn Ukiyoe and was named after the third *Toyokuni* in 1844. He portrayed *Kabuki* actors and beautiful women in his early career, but was unexcelled at producing *Ukie* (landscapes with a three-dimensional quality).

69 Keisai Eisen
Ukiyoe artist. (1790–1848). Studied drawing even as a young child, later apprenticed to *Kikukawa Eizan,* an Ukiyoe artist. His body of work includes many portraits of prostitutes and *geisha.* Reportedly, he died suddenly after struggling with a lung disease for about three years.

70 Utagawa Toyokuni
Ukiyoe artist. (1769–1825). Born in Edo, apprenticed to *Utagawa Toyoharu,* the originator of the Utagawa School, who educated many excellent Ukiyoe artists of that school. His Ukiyoe portraits of *Kabuki* actors and beautiful women were popular, and he also produced illustrations for book covers.

71 Utagawa Hiroshige
Ukiyoe artist of the later Edo Period. (1797–1858). Born into the *Ando* family, in 1811 he became an apprentice of *Utagawa Toyohiro* and was given the name Utagawa Hiroshige the following year. Particularly talented at portraits of beautiful women and *Kabuki* actors, he later gained popularity by producing picture books, landscapes, caricatures, and so on. He is the most prominent among the Ukiyoe artists of the Utagawa school, and in the field of Ukiyoe landscapes he shares the popularity of *Katsushika Hokusai.*

72 Utagawa Yoshiiku
Also known as *Ochiai Yoshiiku* (1813–1904). He began drawing in 1854, and studied under *Utagawa Kuniyoshi.* He produced many portraits of *Kabuki* actors and beautiful women, and even drew historical scenes. Although his pen name was Utagawa, few of his works were signed *Utagawa Yoshiiku;* many were signed *Ochiai Yoshiiku.*

REFERENCES

Akutsu, Kunio. *Nyuyoku Kenko-ho* (bathing for health). Kodansha, October 30, 1978 (the first printing), May 30, 1983 (the second printing) .

Kojima, Hiroo. *Furo To Kenko* (bath and health). Chisan Shuppan, 1976.

Oshima, Yoshio. *Onsen Ryoho* (a hot spring cure). Sogen-sha, 1956.

Watanabe, Hidefumi. *Onsenburo, Sauna no hairikata de konnani utsukushiku naru* (hot springs, sauna make you more beautiful). Kobunsha, 1986.

Japan Health Development Foundation. *Kurhaus.* Tokuma Communications, 1987.

Noguchi, Fuyuto. *Onsen-gayoi* (visiting hot springs). Asuka Kikaku, March 10, 1986.

Noguchi, Fuyuto, *Ryoyo Onsen* (hot springs for cure treatment). Hoikusha, October 5, 1981 (the first printing), October 1, 1986 (the second printing).

Hatta, Osamu. *Onsen wa doshite kikuka* (reasons for the efficacies of hot springs). Kanahara Shuppan, 1960.

The FORUM on Thermalism in Japan Jikko Iinkai (executive Committee). *The FORUM on Thermalism in Japan Kinen-shi* (The FORUM on thermalism in Japan Commemorative Journal).

INAX Corp. *Dai-san Kukan* (the third space), a quarterly magazine by INAXSITE Jigyobu.

Kanner, Catherine of INAX Corp. *The Book of the Bath.* Tosho Shuppan, December 12, 1987 (the first printing), April 10, 1990 (the fourth printing).

Ikeuchi, Osamu. *Seiyo Onsen Jijo* (Western hot springs). Kajima Shuppan-kai, December 20, 1989.

Takeda, Katsuzo. *Furo To Yu No Hanashi* (tales of baths and hot springs). Hanawa Shobo, April 15, 1967 (the first printing), June 30, 1990 (the sixth printing).

Japan Spa Association. *Spas in Japan.* June 1, 1983.

Oba, Osamu, *Furo no Hanashi* (story of bath). Kajima Shuppan.

"ONSEN" THE HOT SPRING GLOSSARY

Japan is blessed with an abundance of hot springs, which have long been used in treatments and cures for various illnesses and injuries. Remarks on these practices abound in the ancient *Nihon Shoki* and *Fudoki* texts.

Many people enjoy visiting particular hot springs whose waters have been noted as particular cures: those for injuries to the skin, for palsy, for the discomforts of pregnancy, for beauty, and so on.

Due to the contemporary preferences for nature, leisure, health, and amenities, a new kind of health resort has recently come into being. These kurhauses, as they are known, have opened one after another during the past few years under the leadership of the Japan Health Development Foundation. The familiar hot spring resorts of the past are being transformed into multi-functional recreation facilities.

What is a Hot Spring?

The Hot Spring Act of 1948 defines hot springs as the following: "A hot spring contains hot water, mineral water, steam and natural gases other than those which are mainly made up of hydrocarbons, the temperature of which at the point at which the spring water leaves the earth is over 25°C or which contains more than the minimum amount of any of the 19 standard components. In Japan, the minimum temperature of a hot spring is over 25°C, whereas in Europe this is 20°C and in the United States 21°C.

Hot springs occur when steam from underground magma and ground water heated by magma dissolve various substances at high temperatures and pressures. These pressures can be fifty thousand times that of air pressure at the earth's surface, and hot springs can flow for hundreds of years. Hot spring waters contain a wide variety of chemicals and gases, and it is said that no two springs are exactly identical. Their properties and efficacies differ subtly according to the kind and amount of the substances in their waters.

Minimum Amounts of Dissolved Substances

According to the Hot Springs Act
(mg/kg unless otherwise noted)

Total dissolved solids	1000
Free carbon dioxide (CO_2)	250
Lithium ions (Li^+)	1
Strontium ions (Sr^{2+})	10
Barium ions (Ba^{2+})	5
Iron ions (Fe^{2+}, Fe^{3+})	10
Manganese ions (Mn^{2+})	10
Hydrogen ions (H^+)	1
Bromine ions (Br^-)	5
Iodine ions (I^-)	1
Fluorine ions (F^-)	2
Hydroarsenic acid ($HAsO_4^{2-}$)	1.3
Metarsenious acid ($HAsO_2^-$)	1
Sulfur (S)	1
Metabolic acid (HBO_2)	5
Metasilicic acid (H_2SO_3)	50
Sodium hydrogen carbonate ($NaHCO_3$)	340
Radon (Ra)	20×10^{-10} curies
Radium salts (as Ra)	1×10^{-8} curies

The Properties and Efficacies of Hot Spring Bathing

The efficacies of bathing in general as described in the preceding chapter, which are due to such factors as hydrostatic pressure and buoyancy, are of course shared by hot spring bathing. However, the precise efficacies of hot spring bathing are more significant than those of hot water bathing, and vary widely. Four categories of effects produced by hot spring bathing or drinking hot spring waters are listed below, and then discussed individually.

—**the effects of chemical components**
—**the effects on health normalization**
—**the effects of a change of air**
—**the effects on beauty**

1. The effects of chemical components
The chemicals contained in hot spring water are absorbed by the body through the skin and the respiratory organs. The carbon dioxide of a carbonated spring, the hydrogen sulfide of a sulfur spring, the sodium ions of a saline spring, and the iron ions of an ion spring are all absorbed through the sebaceous glands which are associated with hair folicles on the skin's surface, and are passed along to the blood vessels. Although most of these substances are eliminated from the body through the lungs via the heart, the small amounts which remain act to stimulate the pituitary gland located in the brain, which controls the secretion of hormones. Thus, various body functions are activated. A wide variety of effects are produced, such as increased appetite, improved blood circulation which prevents arteriosclerosis, and so on.

2. The effects on health normalization
Curiously enough, hot spring bathing affects the control and stabilization of autonomous functions of the nervous system. For example, a hot spring bath can bring a condition of over- or under-secretion of adrenalin into balance.

After a hot spring bath, we are relieved of our stress and irritation along with any sense of enervation or exhaustion, due to the effects of the hot spring on health normalization.

3. The effects of a change of air
The air of a hot spring resort in a natural setting tranquilizes the nerves and improves respiratory functioning. The substances emitted by living plants, especially the fragrant terpene exhaled by a stand of mixed trees, and the anions found in the spray of a rushing stream or a waterfall all produce beneficial effects in the body. Drinking water which is rich in mineral content, and delicious food prepared with fresh marine and mountain ingredients, combine with the change of air to enhance the recovery of both mental and physical functions. The change of air works together with health normalization to reestablish the natural rhythm of the body.

4. The effects on beauty
Carbonate and sulfur springs are known as "hot springs for beauty." Carbonate springs soften the skin, and sulfur breaks down collagen to make the skin smooth. Both act to make the skin more beautiful. Thermotherapy using hot spring waters improves blood circulation in the skin and throughout the body. Nutrients are distributed throughout the skin, and beauty is created from both inside and outside the body.

The Variety of Hot Springs and their Efficacies
1. Simple springs
Simple springs contain various substances in low concentrations. Weak saline springs and weak bicarbonate springs are examples of simple springs. The low concentrations of chemicals do not greatly stimulate the body, and these springs are widely used for recovery from rheumatism, cerebral palsy, problems with the joints, external wounds, and general recuperation following illness. Drinking the waters of such springs benefits the stomach and the intestines and promotes urination.

2. Simple carbonated springs

Simple carbonated springs contain carbonic acid gas, and their temperatures are moderate. Carbonic acid gas acts to dilate the capilaries and other small blood vessels of the skin and mucous membranes, thus improving circulation. Drinking the water of such a spring improves the functioning of the digestive organs and benefits those who suffer from weak digestion and constipation.

3. Bicarbonate springs

Bicarbonate-earth springs

Bicarbonate-earth springs are rich in calcium and magnesium ions, and have a sedative effect. These springs inhibit allergies, chronic skin diseases, hives and inflammations.

Sodium bicarbonate springs

Sodium bicarbonate springs are noted for their beautifying effects. The water smoothes the skin and relieves skin diseases. Drinking these waters enhances stomach and liver functioning.

4. Saline springs

Saline springs are properly called sodium chloride springs, and their waters are characterized by a biting taste. Saline springs are divided into strong and weak versions according to salt concentrations. The former is very effective for keeping warm, while the latter improves chronic rheumatism, cold extremities, bruises, sprains and so on. Drinking these waters benefits the stomach and liver, but imbibing excessive amounts is not good for those with hypertension, heart disease, renal disease or swellings.

5. Sulfate springs

Sodium sulfate springs

Sodium sulfate springs relieve chronic constipation, corpulence, hypertension, external wounds and other ailments.

Plaster (calcium sulfate) springs

Plaster springs produce a sedative effect. They are good for bruises, lacerations, burns, anal fistulae, sprains, skin diseases and so on.

Bitter (magnesium sulfate) springs

Bitter springs produce effects similar to those of sodium sulfate and plaster springs.

Alum (aluminum sulfate) springs

Alum springs are recommended for those suffering from chronic skin diseases and inflammation of the mucous membranes.

6. Iron springs

There are two kinds of iron springs, ferric carbonate springs and ferrous sulfate springs. Poor blood will be improved by drinking from either of these. Many ferric carbonate springs have a strong rust color which is associated with a decline in the quality of the water, so colorless springs have greater efficacies. Ferrous sulfate springs produce better results in terms of enhancing the blood-producing functions of the body.

7. Sulfur springs

Sulfur springs are distinguished by their odor, which is often compared to that of rotten eggs. Sulfur combats poisons, and these springs are good for metal or medicinal poisoning. These waters also soften and dissolve horny substances to improve acne, and are beneficial for cases of chronic bronchiectasis. However, the stimulation is so strong that invalids, the aged, and those with delicate skin are better off avoiding sulfur springs.

8. Acid springs

Acid springs sting the skin, and their antibacterial action improves dermatophytosis, trichomoniasis and scabies. The stimulation is strong enough that acid spring bathing is not recommended for invalids, the aged, and those with delicate skin. However, one treatment for chronic disease uses strong allassotherapy to cause such extreme stimulation that inflammation of the skin can result. This treatment is good for chronic articular rheumatism.

9. Radioactive springs

Radioactive springs include radium springs and radon springs. While radioactivity is present, there are no dangers since radon is a gas which dissipates into the air as soon as the water leaves the ground. The concentration of hydrogen ions and other components in these waters promote urination, so they are beneficial for hyperuricemia, gout, and chronic inflammation of the urinary tract. Radioactive springs are also good for the pituitary and adrenal glands and the reproductive organs. They improve diabetes, also.

10. Japanese Kurhauses

"Kurhaus" is a German word which refers to a health institution. There are about 250 hot spring resorts located in Germany which are equipped for long stays, offering medical treatment, hotel facilities, and provisions for cultural, athletic and recreational activities. A consistent system of medical treatment, recovery and recreation, which also acts as a social security system, has been in operation since the seventeenth or eighteenth century.

In Japan, the Japan Health Development Foundation was established in 1971 and has developed the Japanese kurhaus as a multipurpose hot spring resort. The practices of health spas in other advanced countries have been combined with ancient Japanese balneotherapy, incorporating the results of the latest studies on hot spring bathing, and kinetic physiology and other sciences. There are now 27 kurhauses located throughout Japan.

Variety of Hot Springs According to Substances Dissolved in their Waters

Simple Springs	Simple springs contain less than one gram per kilogram at 25°C of the substances specified in the Hot Spring Act. These springs are divided into many kinds according to their contents.
Carbonate Springs	Carbonate springs contain carbon dioxide (carbonic acid gas) in solution.
Bicarbonate-earth springs	One type of bicarbonate spring, bicarbonate-earth springs contain calcium bicarbonate and magnesium bicarbonate in solution.
Sodium bicarbonate springs	Another type of bicarbonate spring, sodium bicarbonate springs contain sodium bicarbonate in solution.
Saline springs	Saline springs contain sodium choloride (ordinary salt) in solution.
Salfate springs	Sulfate springs fall into four categories: sodium sulfate springs, calcium sulfate (plaster) springs, magnecium sulfate (bitter) springs, and aluminum sulfate (alum) springs.
Iron springs	Iron springs are divided into ferric carbonate springs and ferrous sulfate springs.
Sulfur springs	All sulfur springs contain sulfer in solution. There are two types, one of which contains sulfer as a free hydrogen sulfide in solution and the other of which does not. (In the past, only the latter was referred to as a sulfur spring).
Radioactive springs	Radioactive springs contain radon and radium in solution.

A VARIETY OF BATHING EXPERIENCE

Utaseyu bathing

Exposing sore, stiff muscles to a waterfall of hot spring water stimulates blood circulation and relaxes muscle tension. The warmth of the water and the physical pounding of the waterfall combine to produce a powerful massage effect.

Kakariyu bathing

Hot water splashed over the body before entering a bath tub makes the transition to a hot bath much easier on the body. Blood vessels are dilated, which helps prevent the hot flash or dizziness which might otherwise accompany a rapid rise in blood pressure when entering a hot bath.

Bubble-jet bath

The ultrasound generated when streams of bubbles burst against the body has a warming and massaging effect.

Microbubble-jet bath

With a greater quantity of smaller bubbles, compared to an ordinary bubble-jet bath, the massaging is less intense and the bath produces more of a sedative effect.

Imbibing the waters

Drinking from a hot spring introduces the contents of the water directly to the body. A certain amount of care is recommended since dosage and medicinal effects will vary according to the nature of particular spas.

Bathing on foot

Two pools, each less than knee deep in water, are floored with pebbles. After a stroll around the hot pool, bathers walk around the cold pool—alternating back and forth like this will relieve your mental fatigue.

Fountain bath

This bath is specially equipped to relieve the discomfort of hemorrhoids. The bather sits in a bathing chair and a fountain of hot spa water is directed at the afflicted region, stimulating the blood circulation in that area.

Hot jet bath

Streams of hot spa water jet from the sides of the tub to massage the bather. The massage is similar to that created by an *utaseyu* bath, but the impact of the jet is milder and bathers remain cosily submerged in the hot water.

Whirlpool bath

A whirlpool created in a circular tub massages the entire body, with somewhat less pressure than that offered by a hot jet bath.

Box steam bath

A wooden box encloses the whole body, except the head, in a steam bath. Powerful perspiratory effects can be achieved, and using a box steam bath facilitates the metabolic processes.

Sauna bath

The air in a sauna is dry, and the temperature is a hot 60° to 80°C. Perspiration is intense, and the metabolism is enhanced.

Cold water bath

Situated together with a sauna, the cold water bath is used by those who are ready for a break from the heat of the sauna to cool themselves. The interaction of the sauna and the cold water bath strengthen the body and is beneficial to those who easily catch colds.

Inhaling steam

Breathing the steam of hot spring water in a bath room is good for the respiratory organs and is effective for cases of bronchitis, asthma, and other such illnesses.

Recumbent bathing

Lying in a shallow bath of lukewarm water for an extended period is effective in relieving stress, since the blood vessels expand slowly and circulation is promoted. This style of bathing also has a sedative effect and helps one to sleep well.

Inhaling micro-mist spa waters

In a special room, a fine mist of natural hot spring water made up of tiny droplets 45 to 60 microns in diameter can be inhaled to introduce the water to the body through the respiratory system.

Immersion bathing

Soaking the entire body up to the neck in water between 40° and 42°C regulates the blood pressure, stimulates perspiration and facilitates metabolic processes.

INDEX

A

Akechi-buro   108, 110
Akechi Mitsuhide   108
Alvin Toffler   11
Ando Hiroshige   123, 167
Andree Putman   42, 73
Arima   102

B

Bakufu   108
Basil Hall Chamberlain   102, 126
BATHCRIN   133, 134
BATHCRIN Bathherb   134
Bathing Additives   133
Bathing and Beautiful Skin   130
Bathing to Recover a Healthy
   Rhythm of Life   132
Boy's Day   130
Buoyancy   129

C

Celine   96
Ceramic sand bath   89
Chinpi   134
Citoron hot Bath   130

D

Daikoku-Yu   117
Dochu Hizakurige   123
Dogo   102
Dojo Nyuyokuno Zu   143

E

Edo Nyuyoku Hyaku Sugata   122, 123
Eizo Shiina   36

F

Fugo-buro   120, 121
Furo   104, 118, 120
Furo-taki   173
Furo-yakata   108, 109, 110, 114,
   116, 118
Fuzoku Gaho   113

G

Geisha   159
Geta   122
Go   114
Goemon-buro   120, 122, 123
Gyouzui Bijin   161, 162, 163

H

Hakka   134
Hamaboufu   134
Hanae Mori   96
Harai   102
High Temperature Baths   128,
   131, 132
Higo Zuiki   175
Higozuiki Shohen   160
Hirota Tatsu   145
Hiroshige   155
Hiunkaku   116, 117
Hojo Masako   108
Hokkekyo Mandara Ezu   108, 110
Hokke-mandara   110
Hokusai   155
Honganji   116, 117
Honpoji   110
Hydrostatic pressure characteris-
   tics   128, 129

I

Ideyu   136
Ideyu No Ame   147
Imamura Shiko   146
Imayou-nenju-gyouji-no-uchi   171
Irikomi   172
Irimoya-zukuri   109
Ishi-buro   104
Issey Miyake   90
Ito Shinsui   144
Izumisa Version   157

J

Japanese Iris   130
Joushin   144

K

Junji Kawada   20
Junko Koshino   96
Jurakudai   117

Kaburagi Kiyokata   152
Kaichu Nenju Gyouji   174
Kajiwara Hisako   147
kakari-yu   108, 111, 116, 118
Kama-buro   106, 107
Kami   137
Kamiarai Bijin   166
Kamitsure   134
Kanazawa Kenko   122
Kano Tanyu   113
Karahafu   108, 109, 110, 111,
   114, 116, 117
Karasu-tengu   120
Keisai Eisen   160, 174, 175
ken   109
Kengu Irikomi Sento-shinwa   115
Kenzo   96
Kibyoshi   115
Kimono   158, 166.
Kirizuma   109, 110, 117
Kitagawa Utamaro   157
Kitamandokoro   156
Kita-san   120, 123
Kobayakawa Kiyoshi   149
Kobayashi Kokei   136, 137
Kotto-shu   122
Kuge   112
Kunio Yanagida   104
Kurhaus   66, 69, 70
Kusuri-yu   115
Kyoudouburo   160

L

Luke warm Baths   129, 130, 132

M

Manjuin   121
Masako Hayashi   23

MCH Research Institute   24
Medicated Baths   134
Meiji Jibutsu Kigen   113
Minami House Design and Co., Ltd.
   30
Minamotono Yoritomo   108
Misogi   102
Miyako-meisho-zue   107
Morgan   42, 73
Muro   104
Mushiburo   153, 172
Mugi-buro   120, 121
Myoshinji   108, 110, 111, 116, 118

N
Nagoyajo Taimenjo Jodan-no-ma-
   no Goten Shoji Koshibarie   113
Nakamura Teiji   148
Natsuno-hino Gyozui   174
Ne-yu   70
Nicole   96, 97
Ninai-buro   122, 123
Nishi Honganji   116

O
Oatsurae Tousegonomi   166
Ochiai Rofu   151
Ogura Yuki   141, 142, 143
Okada Architectural Office   78
Onishiki size   157, 158, 159, 161,
   162, 165, 166, 167, 171
Onnayu Fuzokuzu   171
Onna-yu-no Bijinga   175
Otoshi   123
Oukakudai   116, 117, 118
O-yu   104

P
Pittori Piccoli   16

R
Rakuchu-rakugai-zu Byobu   112, 113
Ralph Lauren   96
Renoma   96

S
Sana   121
Santo Kyoden   115, 122
Sawa Kojin   153
Seirou Nanakomachi, Ogiyanai
   Takigawa   157
Senchu-buro   176
Senkyu   134
Sento   108, 112, 114, 122
Sento Fuzoku Zu   160
Sento Shinwa   172, 173, 176
Seyoku   108, 110, 112
Shin-yoshiwara   157, 158, 173
Shira-yu   115
Shoubuyu   152, 165
Shogi   114
Shoin   78, 114
Shuji Miura   11
Soba   159
Soushi Araikomachi   161
Sue-buro   120
Sukiya   78
Sunoko-bari   108, 118

T
Takayama Tatsuo   140
Tatami   51, 106, 107, 113, 114
Teppo-buro   120, 122, 123
Thalassotherapy   89
Thermal characterlistics   128
The Slimming Efficacy of Bathing
   131
Thierry Mugler   73
Thyunzyoubou Tyougen   104, 108
Tobikomi-buro   121
Todaiji   104, 108, 109, 110, 114
Todaiji Garan   104
Todana-buro   112, 113, 118, 119
Tokaidochu Hizakurige   120
Tokyo fuzoku-shi   115
Torii   114
Touki   134
Toyotomi Hideyoshi   156
Tsuchida Bakusen   138

Tsuji-buro   122, 123

U
Ukiyoburo   167, 169
Ukiyoburo Hitokuchi-monku
   167, 169
Ukiyo Juroku Musashi   159
Ukiyotokei Juniji, Sarunokoku   162
Ushida Findlay Partnership   24
Utagawa Hiroshige   167, 169
Utagawa Kunisada   158, 159, 161,
   162, 165, 166, 172, 173, 176
Utagawa Toyokuni   161, 163
Utagawa Yoshiiku   171
Utase-yu   70, 71, 72

W
Wakansenyo-shu   122
Whirlpool   16, 24, 30, 39, 41, 56,
   57, 59, 60, 66, 67, 68, 70, 72, 88,
   89

Y
Yase   106, 107
Yaji-san   120, 123
Yoji Yamamoto   96
Yokujo   141, 142
Yokushitsu   140, 151
Yosemune-zukuri   117
Yoshinobu Ashihara   51
Yoshiwara   155
Yoshiwaratokei Minokoku, Hiru
   Yotsu   158
Yuagari   149
Yuagari Bijin-ga   157, 158, 159
Yuami   145
Yuami Shite   148
Yuna   112, 113, 138
Yuno Yado   146
Yve Saint Laurent   73

Z
Zakuro-guchi   114, 115, 167, 169
Zegaibo-eshi   120, 121

PHOTOGRAPH CREDITS

The author and publisher wish to thank the museums, galleries, and private collectors for permitting the reproduction of works in their collections.

All photographs of Ukiyoe have been suppllied by Mr. Kazuhiko Fukuda.